Illness as Method

Beckett, Kafka, Mann, Woolf, and Eliot

Jayjit Sarkar
Raiganj University, India

Series in Literary Studies

VERNON PRESS

Copyright © 2020 Vernon Press, an imprint of Vernon Art and Science Inc, on behalf of the author.

All rights reserved. No part of this publication may be reproduced, stored in a retrieval system, or transmitted in any form or by any means, electronic, mechanical, photocopying, recording, or otherwise, without the prior permission of Vernon Art and Science Inc.

www.vernonpress.com

In the Americas:
Vernon Press
1000 N West Street,
Suite 1200, Wilmington,
Delaware 19801
United States

In the rest of the world:
Vernon Press
C/Sancti Espiritu 17,
Malaga, 29006
Spain

Series in Literary Studies

Library of Congress Control Number: 2019938496

ISBN: 978-1-62273-805-2

Also available: 978-1-62273-635-5 [Hardback]; 978-1-62273-732-1 [PDF, E-Book]

Product and company names mentioned in this work are the trademarks of their respective owners. While every care has been taken in preparing this work, neither the authors nor Vernon Art and Science Inc. may be held responsible for any loss or damage caused or alleged to be caused directly or indirectly by the information contained in it.

Every effort has been made to trace all copyright holders, but if any have been inadvertently overlooked the publisher will be pleased to include any necessary credits in any subsequent reprint or edition.

To all those around the world

who are trying to find a method in their illness

"nobody wants an anonymous illness"

-Anatole Broyard

Table of contents

	Foreword by Pramod K Nayar	*ix*
	Prologue	*xiii*
	Acknowledgments	*xvii*
	Introduction	*xix*
Chapter 1	**The Dys-abled Players** **of Samuel Beckett's** *Endgame*	1
Chapter 2	**The Circumcised Body** **of Franz Kafka's Select Letters**	15
Chapter 3	**'Connoisseurship… of Disease'** **and Thomas Mann's** *Death in Venice*	27
Chapter 4	**'Undiscovered Countries'** **with Virginia Woolf's** *On Being Ill*	39
Chapter 5	**'Connect Nothing with Nothing'** **in T. S. Eliot's** *The Wasteland*	49
	Epilogue	*59*
	Pathography	*67*
	Index	*73*

Foreword

Linking disease and its adjuncts, such as therapeutic and recuperative, with aesthetics, Jayjit Sarkar offers a fresh approach to the European modernists: Mann, Eliot, Beckett, Kafka, Woolf. Positioning the body, especially the vulnerable body, at the centre of literary pathography, Sarkar also seeks a movement beyond this immediate corporeality when he speaks of the 'unmechanised and porous *body* without fixed contours' seeking, he says, to explore the 'porous boundaries that exist between body, illness and writing'.

For Sarkar the famous, or notorious, modernist alienation has a pathographic equivalent:

> The lived experience of an impaired body, the body-in-itself, becomes symptomatic of the general human condition in modern times. The incapacity to interact and communicate with the surroundings makes those bodies apprehensive of the inter-subjective and inter-corporeal acknowledgement necessary for survival.

The modernist angst, then, argues Sarkar in an innovative reading that recalls Tim Armstrong's work on the body and technology in modernism (which Sarkar cites early in his own study), is the effect of a pathography between body, mind and medical knowledge, and therefore 'psychosomatic'.

Sarkar's attention to tropes and metaphors in complex authors like Kafka generates innovative readings as when, for instance, he points out the sense of 'desubjectivication' as a Jewish *and* sick body in Kafka's letters. Thomas Mann, writes Sarkar, 'juxtaposes biological decay, repressed desire and *dépaysement—* the state of being in a foreign, unfamiliar country' in the body/person of Aschenbach. Disease, which draws our attention to our corporeality, is 'a mode of emancipation towards knowledge'. Woolf, says Sarkar, writes *out* from the body, what he terms 'ex-scribe'. Eliot's Wasteland, argues Sarkar, is inhabited by diseased bodies that can only 'connect nothing with nothing' – they are not engaged with the urban spaces they occupy but are 'victims of gross mechanization'. Making much of 'connect nothing with nothing' (which contradicts the Bloomsbury ethos of 'only connect', made famous by E.M. Forster), Sarkar argues that due to illness, the connection between the body and the world is disrupted. The disease 'transforms the coherent subject and alienates him/her from the *a priori* of the life-world'.

The modernists, with the wide range of themes of suffering, angst and neuroses, are complicated figures at best. It becomes difficult, as Sarkar appears to recognize, to 'formulate them in a phrase'. Hence Sarkar's strategy of *not* reducing questions and themes of the bodily to just the corporeal body is a clever one. The attention to ontology and corporeality that intersects via dis-ease with the phenomenological and even the metaphysical enables Sarkar to avoid the pitfalls of biomedical reductionism.

While some attention to biomedical care and institutions of such care – disease has a social dimension, as we now know – would have located the above angle within a more historicized context, one would be churlish to hold this as a negative feature of Sarkar's work. When speaking of alienation (in Eliot) or social situations where desire (Mann) and anxiety (Woolf) are played out within the body but also extend beyond it, Sarkar seems clearly aware of the social imaginaries that hedge and circumscribe the diseased body.

Centring the body in modernism, as Sarkar has done, enables him to return to the individual at the heart of modernist concerns. For instance, like Cassandra Laity's work on decadent bodies and new modes of perception in modernism, Sarkar alerts us to the alternative frames within which the body, both healthy and sick, was viewed in the period. In this aspect, Sarkar's work is an important intervention, for it shows and develops an *approach* to the modernists, but is not restricted to just Eliot/Pound/Woolf. A therapeutic modernism appears to be at work in Sarkar's study.

Adapting the work of a wide variety of thinkers across disciplines as diverse but related as philosophy and literary studies – Sontag, Merleau-Ponty, Nancy, Scarry, among others – serves Sarkar well. He is able to address the body in all its multiplicities (with less attention paid, perhaps, to mental health issues). He is able to foreground the thematic of relationships, including desiring ones, in the corporeal. Finally, he is able to demonstrate how metaphors and tropes – in places the work reminded me of *Metaphors We Live By* – draw upon body images and bodily conditions. Whether these metaphors were a response to the amplified mechanization of the period is a moot point, and Sarkar's work definitely implies this argument.

Sarkar's book, pithy, poignant in parts due to its material, and pertinent is an important contribution to modernism studies but will also be relevant to fields such as the medical and health humanities. Close reading and philosophical meditations that are grounded in representations, language and discourses make the work a pleasure to read. The insights, drawing upon numerous theoretical frames, are interesting and challenging for they do call upon us to re-evaluate the modernists.

Pramod K Nayar
Department of English
The University of Hyderabad, India

Prologue

This work questions the problematic connection between illness and modernity: complicated negotiations involving the body both in its physicality and phenomenology and the poetics and praxiality of illness. The project, which is predominantly conceptual in nature for it does not see illness solely as a clinical-physical category (with heavy leanings on medical sciences) but perspectivizes its phenomenology and pathographical limits and manifestations, lateralizes on its critical correspondences with a select band of modernist texts ranging from Virginia Woolf to Samuel Beckett. My work unearths different other 'possibilities' of illness without denying its (quite natural) association with morbidity, pain, suffering, dying and death. It looks at illness and its effects on different bodies phenomenologically with the help of some twentieth-century philosophers namely, Martin Heidegger, Jean Luc-Nancy, Maurice Merleau-Ponty, Jean Paul Sartre, Emmanuel Levinas et al. The book locates these phenomenological understandings in my reading of some of the important literary works of early twentieth-century Europe— five different literary works of five different genres (poetry, drama, fiction, non-fiction and epistles) — critiquing the relevance of the phenomenological body in the literary and narrative world of the texts. My work chooses Samuel Beckett's *Endgame*, Franz Kafka's letters, Thomas Mann's *Death in Venice*, Virginia Woolf's *On Being Ill*, and T. S. Eliot's *The Wasteland* within the aesthetico-philosophical space and the epistemic dialogism that modernist aesthetics implies and spouses.

Modernity and its contemporary disability find their just representation in the post-Holocaust-like situation of Samuel Beckett's *Endgame*. The first chapter titled 'The Dys-abled Players of Samuel Beckett's *Endgame*' looks into the disabled characters, their impaired bodies in the play, to disembed the hermeneutic continuity and see those bodies in their phenomenological materiality; it would mean going back to the internal structure of pain, suffering and disability. 'Circumcised Body of Franz Kafka's Select Letters', the second chapter, investigates Kafka's epistolary conversations which are also in a way his body-writings. Kafka's imagining of his body— an 'overdetermined' body racially and medically infested with different meanings— was a part of the early twentieth-century anti-Semite *weltanschauung*. Such discourses, especially, medical discourses, were generated to re-produce the Jewish body as abnormal, diseased and deviant— the abject 'other'. Kafka and his bleeding body with all its flesh and blood and its embodiedness anticipate the condition of the Jewish body during the time of *Shoah*. And in this 'somatic turn', Kafka emerges as a brilliant study of the history of the flesh and the history in the flesh, a perfect paradigm of how that demonstrates in the twentieth-century the crises in civilization and how that leads to the crises of representation. The third chapter entitled 'Connoisseurship...of Disease and Thomas Mann's *Death in Venice*' juxtaposes biological decay, repressed desire and *dépaysement*— the state of being in a foreign, unfamiliar country. In the novella, the beauty of the Venetian city and the destruction of Gustav von Aschenbach's forbidden love for Tadzio are closely interwoven. Set at the backdrop of the cholera epidemic illness becomes a metaphor of 'a new susceptibility to the erotic' and the Dionysian impulses ('*Kunsttriebe*'). Playing on the dichotomies of modern life with its divided aims, Mann weaves a narrative based on modern metaphors and illness— illness as metaphors and metaphors as illness. Like the Romantics, Mann regards illness and dying as both an end and a mode of emancipation. The fourth chapter – 'Undiscovered Countries with Virginia Woolf's *On Being Ill*' – seeks to validate the perspective of the invalid and the recluse. In the essay Woolf traces the journey of a recluse who in illness withdraws from the daily humdrum of life, from the hustle and bustle of the city of health to a room of one's own: a room which allows one to reflect on things around, and see the world both inside and outside in different light. Here, the pre-reflective involvement with the world gives way to a more contemplative and meditative way of looking. Like *epoché*, illness can become a tool for philosophical enquiry. The Romantic empathy of sitting and hearing 'each other groan' is substituted by a modernist disjuncture and 'disinterestedness'. It enables the pensive pathological being to challenge the discourses of modern urban existence driven by machines. The Chapter Five titled 'Connect Nothing with Nothing in T. S. Eliot's *The Waste Land*' (re)reads the most representative poem of the time in which we find a blind transgendered speaker lamenting on the sickness of modern life figured through a king who is suffering from an undiagnosed disease and who fishes by a polluted stream. *The Waste Land* epitomizes modernism's reaction against modernity. The poem is analysed as a pathological narrative— a narrative which diagnoses the problem of alienation, disjuncture, sterility, mechanicality, fragmentation and breakdown of communication and as prognosis prescribes a new vision of centre.

The overarching question, however, in all these remains the same: in what way pathology and poetics tend to overlap? The effort to locate the zone of indistinction between the poetics of pathology and pathology of poetics can be exhaustive but not unfruitful; its understanding requires a phenomenological and psychoanalytical enquiry into the question of body, illness and writing. How the body speaks through illness and how illness speaks through writing? This work perceives the body as emaciated, incompetent, impotent and painful and deals with the complex of mind-body-matter and the mysterious 'happening' (*Geschehen*) of human existence. It raises some essential and existential questions pertaining to the twentieth-century human condition in the light of a generic reading of modernism in general and the modern literature in particular— demonstrating how pain transmutes into an art form. Through a pregnant hyphenation of literature and/as pathography the texts in questions and under separate chapter heads rethink the premises of modernity, the body as a process, illness as aesthetics of doing and happening, interrogating the foundations of art and pain, writing and writhing, expressions and experiences. My work problematises illness in the making and the unmaking of literature as poiesis, pathology, 'patient', and pathography.

Acknowledgments

I extend my heartfelt gratitude to my PhD supervisor Ranjan Ghosh, Department of English, University of North Bengal, India whose continuous intellectual and moral support has enabled me to undertake and accomplish this meticulous project. His *presence* is something I always cherish. He has always been an inspiration for me. I am grateful to Prof. Pramod K Nayar, Department of English, University of Hyderabad, India for taking out time from his busy schedule and write the foreword for the book. I am thankful to my friend Jagannath Basu for his valuable inputs and suggestions. I am also indebted to Pavanbir Kaur, Prasun Banerjee, Binay Kumar Patel, Sudip Khasnobish, and Bipransh Kumar Tiwari for their continuous support and much-needed motivation. This book germinated from my PhD dissertation 'Poetics of Pathology: Modernity, Illness and a Select Reading of Twentieth-Century European Literature (1910-1960)' so I must also thank the administration of University of North Bengal for allowing me to publish my PhD work. I am much obliged to my family especially my father and my brother and for their incessant support while I was doing my work. My heart goes out to all those who, like my mother, suffer for a long time and finally succumb after a strong fight over which they have little or practically no control.

Introduction

I am the illness and the medical intervention, I am the cancerous cell and the grafted organ, I am the immuno-depressive agents and their palliatives...

-Jean Luc-Nancy *L'Intrus*

Illness is not known; it is suffered, and similarly the body is revealed by the illness and likewise suffered by consciousness.

-Jean Paul Sartre *Being and Nothingness*

Thinking through the ill body

Is there a possibility of something as despicable as illness becoming a mode of philosophical tool? Is there a possibility where illness can open up new avenues of looking at life? Is there a possibility of illness pulling us out of our deep slumber, our state of ignorance? And is there a possibility that all these possibilities can lead us to a renewed conception of illness as distinguished from illness being oft thought as antithetical to the *bliss* of health and life? My work looks *patient*-ly for all such possibilities which can enable us to see illness with a difference. I am committed to unearthing different other 'possibilities' of illness without denying its (quite natural) association with morbidity, pain, suffering, dying and death. The *bliss* I just referred to is a state of oblivion which this book is going to diagnose as health; it is from which prognosis comes in the form of illness. My work tries to capture such reverse attitudes by moving away from the predominant logical scientism. It will rather look at illness and its effects on different bodies phenomenologically with the help of some twentieth-century philosophers namely, Martin Heidegger, Jean Luc-Nancy, Maurice Merleau-Ponty, Jean Paul Sartre, and Emmanuel Levinas. I will try to locate these phenomenological understandings in my reading of some of the important literary works of early twentieth-century Europe. In trying to understand the 'poetics of pathology' in modern times, I have engaged with five different literary works of five different genres— poetry, drama, fiction, non-fiction and epistles—critiquing the relevance of the phenomenological body in the literary and narrative world of the texts. These texts turn into what Anne Hunsaker Hawkins has called "pathography" (plural, pathographies)[1].

Modernist aesthetics with its tension, disability and entropy become a good hunting ground for connections building between art and the fragility of immature psychosis. Psychology, physiology and literature in their generic manifestations have a close and effective connect with pathology— illness, as a state of body and mind corresponding with the state of art. Aesthetics problematically straddles both the mind that creates and the mind that suffers. The philosophers of the twentieth-century in question have thought out the psycho-physical dynamics through engagements in phenomenology, poiesis, materiality, aesthetics of flesh, embodiedness and other related discourses. The artist within modernist aesthetics mind holds philosophy and literature at the crossroad of a frantic traffic between a host of disciplines and complexes of critical interests. So the choice of Franz Kafka, T. S. Eliot, Virginia Woolf, Thomas Mann, and Samuel Beckett within the aesthetico-philosophical space and the epistemic dialogism that modernist aesthetics implies and spouses, at the premise of a theory-praxis double bind where modernist aesthetics through my work, comes to bear out its issues as vexed as body and embodiedness, pain and pathology, health and heathwiseness in the making of a certain kind of literature.

The vulnerability of the body intensified during the first half of the twentieth century. The chasm between an *able* body and a *disable* body was narrowed down to such an extent that they, quite often, overlapped. The 'somatic turn' that the century took exposed the body to dizzying new heights built on the structures of industrialization and urbanization and these structures concomitantly brought with them the madness of sciences and pseudo-sciences. The politics of eugenics, demonization of the other, racial segregation and cleansing, were all meted out on the contemporary bodies. The effects of the Great Wars or what F. R. Leavis would call the 'great hiatus' were as much psychological as corporeal. The kind of somatic vulnerability that this age witnessed was unprecedented. The modern ill body was a reaction against such adventures and misadventures of *modernity*. Illness then becomes one of the symptoms of a body revolting against the lunacy of contemporary biopolitics. The *hubris* of the Enlightenment and its project of colonizing the 'other' paved the way for a new kind of politics which can be traced in not only the colonial and imperial relationships but also in philosophy, literature,

---

[1] Anne Hunsaker Hawkins, *Reconstructing Illness: Studies in Pathography*, (Indiana, Purdue University Press, 1999), 1. Hawkins defines pathography as writing that "describes personal experiences of illness, treatment, and sometimes death."

Introduction

the medical sciences, the eugenic studies, economics and the politics of the day. Bodies were either seen piling upon each other in trenches or lying wounded in hospitals or revolting against the politics of violence on streets. Bodies in art and fascist propaganda alike were pushed to their limits and, sometimes even beyond. Such extremities are quite evident in F. T. Marinetti's harrowing Futurist proclamation, "War is beautiful because it imitates the dreamt-of metalization of the human body... because it combines the gunfire, the cannonades, the cease-fire, the scents, and the stench of putrefaction into a symphony"[2]. No age witnessed the blurring of physical pain and psychological trauma in such a manner the way Modern period did. And by doing so the-spirit-of-the-age, though unwittingly, challenged the very fundamental of Cartesian dualism: the body and the mind as two distinct entities. The modernist *angst* was undoubtedly psychosomatic in nature.

Illness, as perceived in the first half of the twentieth century, was very different from that of the preceding ages. For the first time, the perception of medicine as a science was visibly observed. The modern medical technology enabled us to penetrate the skin and locate the disease in the human body. The whole body was no more held accountable for the problem and consequently, the prevalent idea of associating disease with disposition was thwarted. Although the location of the disease and in a way illness was one of the highlights of the age, the spirit of the age failed to prevent illness, disease, and impairment from becoming the dominant metaphors across art and culture. These metaphors became the characteristics of the (de)generation itself. And, hence not surprisingly, the entire modernist poetics and aesthetics is replete with such images. The tendency of connecting modern 'literariness' with such metaphors is a commonplace thing in various new modernist readings.

In this modern project of locating the disease onto a particular section of the human body the sufferer and the agency of the sufferer were somewhere sidelined. The disease became more important than the patient; the part became more important than the whole. The entire focus was now on the disease and the body part(s) affected by the disease. The sufferer was rendered a voiceless, inert being— a mere subject of many rigorous medical examinations. The modern human body was thus fragmented, examined, re-examined, commodified, formed and re-formed, all under strict medical surveillance.

---

[2] F.T. Marinetti, "Manifesto Concerning the Ethiopian Colonial War" quoted in Walter Benjamin, *The Work of Art in the Age of Mechanical Reproduction* (London, Penguin Books Limited, 2008), 36-7.

The self-conscious modernist work-of-art can roughly be compared to the body which becomes self-conscious during illness. The former calls for attention to the form while in the latter, the hitherto absent-body (re)appears and seeks attention for itself or its part(s). The body *presences* itself in illness and disappears in health. In illness, the body is perceived *as* body and not merely *res extensa*. This self-reflexivity of the body in illness seems quite similar to that of the self-reflexive nature of the signifier and the form in modernist anti-art. The 'reality' in modernist art was basically 'corpo-reality'; but this corpo-reality was not located in a 'respectable' body of baroque art but rather in fragmented bodies, traumatic bodies, alienated bodies, abject bodies and machinic bodies of the time. Illness and disease then become not only the predominant metaphors of the period but also the mode via which the (fractured) reality was perceived. It blurred the line between the art of diagnosis and the diagnosis of art. Modern literature in particular and modern art in general then can be viewed as the record of symptoms of the age and, also in many cases, the prescription.

The likely comparison between the modernist nostalgia for a 'perfect past' and the overarching desire for and reminiscence of a 'perfect health' cannot be ignored too. Looking at the modernist longing for the past in strictly pathological terms (to the French counterpart *la maladie du pays* and the German counterpart *das Heimweh*), Tammy Clewell goes on to locate this nostalgic longing onto the bodies of various subjects: "soldiers, mothers, the privileged, middle classes, and dispossessed, colonial subjects, city dwellers, and artists" for different objects of longing: "hometowns, loved ones, maternal comforts, country houses, urban entertainments, primitive cultures, and artistic practices."[3] Emphasizing on the *algia* part Clewell makes an interesting study of modernist 'nostalgia' as a corporeal phenomenon. Similarly, from a phenomenological point of view, illness exerts a *telic demand*[4]— an overwhelming longing to be free from illness, to be in idyllic 'perfect health'. Going beyond the painful *here* and *now*, both modernist aesthetics and illness bring forth nostalgia as a mode of resisting as well as subverting the current state of being. The conflation of the modernist *angst* of modernity and the corporeal *angst* of illness becomes one of the highlights of the age.

Modernism and its biopolitical regimes of institutionalization, medicalization and eugenic theories led to the rise of a whole new narrative not only in literature but cultural theory in general. The whole paradigm was corporeal-

---

[3] Tammy Clewell, *Modernism and Nostalgia: Bodies, Locations, Aesthetics*, (New York, Palgrave Macmillan, 1993),10.
[4] Drew Leder, *The Absent Body*, (Chicago, The University Press of Chicago, 1990), 77.

Introduction xxiii

ized, or, rather, phenomenologically speaking, *körpor*-realized. Tim Armstrong points out that "modernism is characterised by the desire to intervene in the body; to render it part of modernity by techniques which may be biological, mechanical or behavioural"[5].These interventions although often had contradictory consequences on different bodies. Even Virginia Woolf, in her essay *On Being Ill*, describes (discussed in detail in Chapter Four) how the diseased body intervenes to produce its own narratives that are not equivalent to those generated by the mind. Such 'intervening' bodies lend a kind of a 'narrative prosthesis' to the entire modernist movement. Guillaume Apollinaire, for instance, while talking about Picasso's *'Les Demoiselles d'Avignon'* writes, "a Picasso studies an object the way a surgeon dissects a corpse"[6]. The modern writing touches upon such extremities; the modern image of the 'patient etherized upon a table' lurks everywhere.

Jean Luc-Nancy calls for such bodily understanding— understanding not about the body, but body itself. In *Corpus*, he calls for writing:

> Let there be writing, not about the body, but the body itself. Not bodihood, but the actual body. Not signs, images, or ciphers of the body, but still the body. This was once a program for modernity, no doubt already it no longer is.[7]

Keeping *il n a pas de hors corpus*[8], that 'there is no outside-body' or its often misconstrued translation 'there is nothing outside of the body' in mind, we can infer that if we are to think about illness and dissemination of illness in twentieth-century European literature, we have to think not merely in terms of philosophy on/of body but body-philosophy.

The dichotomy of corporeal confinement and transcendental mind, of the etherized (the body) and the etherealized (the mind), the *patient* and the im*patient* becomes a metaphor for the modern human condition. And, in such ambiguity, patienthood becomes very symptomatic of "the most quintessentially modernist anxieties— utter lack of agency, affective numbness and inability to discern meaning from language and gesture, the Prufockian impossi-

---

[5] Tim Armstrong, *Modernism, Technology and the Body: A Cultural History*, (Cambridge, Cambridge University Press, 1998), 6.
[6] Guillaume Apollinaire's "On the Subject of Modern Painting" was originally published in Les Soirées de Paris, February 1912; from Leroy C. Breunig, *Apollinaire on Art: Essays and Reviews*, (New York, De Capo Press, 1988)
[7] Jean Luc-Nancy, *Corpus*, (New York, Fordam University Press, 2008), 9.
[8] Ibid, 10.

bility of getting one's mind and tongue in concert ('It is impossible to say just what I mean!'), the psychological paralysis that generates a plethora of inconsequential questions in lieu of actions"[9]. The kind of dilemma and predicament Miss Gee is thrown into in W. H. Auden's 'Miss Gee' highlights the general predicament of the age vis-à-vis the subject-position of being a cancer patient. The harrowing medical gaze the way she is being looked at and the 'treatment' that ensues, become a case-study of modernity and the (in)human condition that it stands for. The poem manifests sheer helplessness at the face of the inhospitable modern medical discourses:

> Doctor Thomas looked her over,
> And then he looked some more;
> Walked over to his wash-basin,
> Said, 'Why didn't you come before?'
>
> Doctor Thomas sat over his dinner,
> Though his wife was waiting to ring,
> Rolling his bread into pellets;
> Said, 'Cancer's a funny thing.
>
> 'Nobody knows what the cause is,
> Though some pretend they do;
> It's like some hidden assassin
> Waiting to strike at you.
>
> 'Childless women get it.
> And men when they retire;
> It's as if there had to be some outlet
> For their foiled creative fire.'
>
> His wife she rang for the servent,
> Said, 'Don't be so morbid, dear';
> He said: 'I saw Miss Gee this evening
> And she's a goner, I fear.'

---

[9] Valerie Lauren Popp, "The Art of Modernist Body", (PhD Diss. University of California, 2011), 4.

> They took Miss Gee to the hospital,
> She lay there a total wreck,
> Lay in the ward for women
> With her bedclothes right up to her neck.
>
> They lay her on the table,
> The students began to laugh;
> And Mr. Rose the surgeon
> He cut Miss Gee in half.
>
> Mr. Rose he turned to his students,
> Said, 'Gentlemen if you please,
> We seldom see a sarcoma
> As far advanced as this.'
>
> They took her off the table,
> They wheeled away Miss Gee
> Down to another department
> Where they study Anatomy.
>
> They hung her from the ceiling
> Yes, they hung up Miss Gee;
> And a couple of Oxford Groupers
> Carefully dissected her knee.[10]

The illness and the metaphors of illness permeate the cultural logic of modernist aesthetics, as Mathew Davidson in his 'By the Road to the Contagious Hospital: Invalid Modernism' lays down how "Matthew Arnold speaks of this strange *disease* of modern life with its *sick* hurry, its divided aims, and Kierkegaard describes unredeemed time as *sickness* unto death. [Fyodor] Dostoevsky's Underground Man, regards excessive consciousness [as] a...genuine absolute *disease*. Charles Baudelaire describes the shock of the modern metropole as a type of nervous *disorder* having its repercussions in the very core of the brain. The artist capable of capturing its effects must be a perpetual *convalescent*. Ezra Pound advocates Imagist economy and clarity as a kind of rhetorical hygiene to cure poetry of *diseased* Victorian excess. [Friedrich] Nietzsche in his later writing on

---

[10] W. H. Auden, 'Miss Gee', *Selected Poems*, (New York, Vintage, 1990), 55-58.

Wagner's music speaks of it as *contagious* and *unhealthy*"[11] (my emphases). The above reference is worth quoting as it helps my case immensely.

Modernism, as Michael Davidson points out, is at once a historical scandal and a contemporary disability[12]. It was a reaction against modernity; it laid the condition for its perpetuation— "a *pharmakon* in serving as 'cure' for modernist malaise as well existing as a disease itself"[13]. The interplay between being patient (numb and impotent) and impatient (reactionary, an escape) makes modernist aesthetics both 'etherized' and 'etherealized', cure and poison, Goebbels' and Picasso's or, what Derrida would call 'the *différance* of difference'. And the modernist ambition of *Gesamtkuntswerk* (a 'total work of art') gave impetus to and laid the condition for these sorts of crises not only in art but in society and politics too. To quote Eliot:

"I am moved by fancies that curled
Around these images, and cling: The notion of some infinitely gentle
Infinitely suffering thing"[14]

All of a sudden "the scientific gaze", as James and Kevin Aho point out in their work, "was turned back on humanity itself. Mankind now became automatized. 'Soul' was rendered into a word whose use indicated sloppy thinking; consciousness was spoken of as an epiphenomenon; mind-stuff was reduced to brain function"[15]. The result of which was instrumentality. The more we try to control and fix an object "by technical procedures, the more we are destined to suffer the anxiety of 'not being at home' (*Unheimlichkeit*)"[16]. My approach, on the other hand, would be of that of *Lebensphilosophie* or of what Wilhelm Dilthey calls *Geisteswissenschaft* (*Geist* means spirit and *Wissenschaft* means science), that is, an approach in

---

[11] Michael Davidson, "By the Road to the Contagious Hospital: Invalid Modernism", 10 November, 2013, https://www.northumbria.ac.uk/static/.../Lect_4_Fashionable_Diseases.pdf, (accessed March 2017).

[12] Ibid. I have discussed this later in detail as the double-edged relationship between modernism and modernity.

[13] Ibid.

[14] T. S. Eliot, 'Prelude', *The Complete Poems and Plays of T. S. Eliot*, (London: Faber and Faber, 1969) L 48-50.

[15] James Aho and Kevin Aho, *Body Matters: A Phenomenology of Sickness, Disease and Illness*, (Plymouth, Lexington Books, 2008), 81.

[16] Ibid, 172.

which one "psychologically enter" into the object, "instead of observing...from a distance— unearthing the lived experience"[17].

My work as already argued would commit to locating illness and its metaphors as it has been disseminated throughout modern European literature in the first half of the twentieth century. The overarching question in all these remains the same: in what way pathology and poetics tend to overlap? The effort to locate the zone of indistinction between the poetics of pathology and pathology of poetics can be exhaustive but not unfruitful, understanding of which requires a phenomenological and psychoanalytical enquiry into the question of body, illness and writing. How the body speaks through illness and how illness speaks through writing? I would prefer arguing much beyond the physical body or the transcendental mind to a more ambiguous area of the phenomenological body— the unmechanised and porous *body* without fixed contours. The body in which we live is also the body *I am*. Hence, an organic understanding of the body is a salient and silent precondition to deal with something which is an indelible part of human existence, involving pain, suffering and decay. Life is but death in disguise. And writing is but life in disguise. Our being makes possible a radical flight through writing— it is not only a mode of emancipation but also a process through which my decaying earthly body speaks and a close reading of which unearths the deep down fissures otherwise unknowable in the daily humdrum. Illness is the royal road to our body and, in a way, to our entire existence. It helps in unpeeling and reducing us to our 'real' self (whatever that means!) for each one of us. My work would deal with such porous boundaries that exist between body, illness, and writing— not so holy a triad.

The understanding of the body both physical and metaphysical is a limited one as they both try to understand the same beyond its 'bodyliness'. A phenomenological study, on the other hand, never takes this 'bodyliness' for granted. Rather, it takes life as it is *lived*. It conceives life, body, illness, decay and death not in isolation but as indistinct from each other. And, they, in turn, are continuously influenced by the world, the worldly and the worldliness. Phenomenology provides me with such a holistic understanding, as opposed to both biological reductionism and metaphysical abstracts; it enables me to appreciate an experience *as* experience. Far from the reductionist view of monism and Cartesian dualism, there is not much of a distinction between the optic, haptic and ontic in Heideggerian understanding of life-world (*Lebenswelt*). The being is always embodied in-the-world and with-the-world.

---

[17] Ibid, 170.

And the understanding of Being demands a proper understanding of this disposition of being.

Heidegger often compares thoughtlessness to analgesia— the state of feeling no pain in the skin. Thinking then and especially meditative thinking (*besinnliches Denken*) in particular becomes an embodied act; feeling pain becomes an important precondition of Being itself. The pathological question, thus, is an important component of the ontological question. In Heidegger, there is not much of a difference between thinking, knowing and acting because 'thinking' as *alētheia* already constitutes 'knowing' and 'acting'— together forming an organised whole. The meditative bodily gesture in illness and disability is very different from a pre-ontological understanding and marks a shift from "the merely ontic to the deeper, more ontological dimensionality of the thoughtful gesture."[18] Illness as an embodied condition helps in the recollection of Being (*anamnēsis*), pulling us out from the amnesia of the anonymous "they" and opening up the more meaningful dimensionality of Being. It changes the way we *presence* ourselves in the world and alters the way we *touch* the "quotidian and everyday to the abstract and rarefied"[19] and consequently, our sensory understanding and the way we think of the world because for Heidegger thinking is always, already haptic. Illness intensifies our sense of touch and deepens our thinking. By opening up the ontic field, it ensues a dialogue of possibilities. Our being-in-the-world (*Dasein*) gets a whole new meaning with illness. The thesis looks for such new dialogues and meanings.

Taking a cue from Rita Charon's concept of 'narrative medicine', a dialogue here will enable us to recognize, absorb, interpret and respond to various generic representations of modernity and illness. The empathetic understanding of the literary artists and their works would allow me "to understand the plight of another by participating in his or her story with complex skills of imagination, interpretation, and recognition"[20]; here in case, the complex skill of phenomenological understanding of the body. I shall read the modern literary works as 'illness narratives' and while doing so will not only be diag-

---

[18] David M. Levin, "Mudra as Thinking: Developing Our Wisdom-of-Being in Gestures and Movements" in *Heidegger and Asian Thought*, ed. Graham Parkes (New Delhi, Motilal Banarasidass, 2018), 245-270. In this chapter while talking about Heidegger's question of Being and gestures Levin refers to Medard Boss' *Existential Foundations of Medicine and Psychology*.
[19] Ibid.
[20] Rita Charon, *Narrative Medicine: Honoring the Stories of Illness*, (New York, Oxford University Press, 2006), 9.

nosing the problem but also look for possible prognoses. The speakers/narrators in these works are like patients seating/lying in front of the physician, im*patient*ly waiting to be heard. Their expectation from the healer is that of a patient hearing. So I, as a reader, like those healers who believe in the importance of narrative medicine, will be patiently hearing their stories and explore the relationship between narrative understanding and the healing process in the manner of Charon. The conversation between the patient and the physician transforms into a storytelling session where the former starts recounting in a narrative, and often in a complicated narrative, of different "words, gestures, physical finds, silences and burdened not with the objective information about the illness but also with the fears, hopes, and implications associated with it"[21] to the latter. In all medical practices, this narrative usually sutured through recounting of the patient, as in the act of psychoanalysis, become a therapeutically central act: as Charon writes "because to find the words to contain the disorder and its attendant worries gives shape to control over the chaos of illness"[22]. And the physician in all this doing, on the other hand, follows

> ... the narrative thread of the story, imagines the situation the teller (the biological, familial, cultural and existential situation), recognize the multiple and often contradictory meanings of the words used and the events described, and in some way enters into and is moved by the narrative world of the patient.[23]

The lived experience of a body in suffering tends to influence the kind of writing it is producing: it finds a vent through the words articulated. The focus would be on the experience of illness and disability as has been disseminated into a literary work and study "the uneasy relationship between words and the life of the body"[24]. My theoretical framework would be to hear those words differently and *patient*-ly. The phenomenological understanding of body, illness and disability, as put forth by continental philosophers like Edmund Husserl, Martin Heidegger, Maurice Merleau-Ponty, Jean-Paul Sartre, Jean Luc-Nancy, et al., will act as the cradle of my study. Their work will provide me with a model and a map for the way I perceive the body as emaciated,

---

[21] Rita Charon, "Narrative Medicine: A Model for Empathy, Reflection, Profession and Trust", *JAMA* 286, no. 15(October 2001): 1898.
[22] Ibid.
[23] Ibid.
[24] **Marilyn Chandler** Mc Entyre, *Patient Poets: Illness from Inside Out*, (San Francisco, University of California Medical Humanities Press, 2012), 1.

incompetent, impotent and painful and, enable me to deal with the complex of mind-body-matter and also the mysterious 'happening' (*Geschehen*) of human existence. Within such philosophic support system, I will raise some essential and existential questions pertaining to the twentieth-century human condition in the light of a generic reading of modernism in general and the modern literature in particular— demonstrating how pain transmutes into an art form.

'Like a patient etherized upon a table': Modernity and Illness

The working definition of 'modernity' (from the Latin *modo* meaning 'now') is a difficult one for various reasons. The concept of modernity is "elusive" and is something which critics are still grappling with[25]. Therefore instead of, concentrating on the *definition* which is quite impossible here, let me concentrate on the very *meaning*— the meaning(s) of modernity. Like illness, my understanding of modernity is less of an event and more of an experience. So what is this experience of modernity and how to characterize the experience of modernity? For this, I have to refer to Marshall Berman who in his Introduction to *All that is Solid Melts into Air: The Experiences of Modernity* refers to a mode of vital experience, "experience of space and time, of the self and others, of life's possibilities and perils— that is shared by men and women all over the world today" and calls this body of experience 'modernity'[26]. To be modern is to belong to a universe of "adventure, power, joy, growth, transformation of ourselves and the world"[27] and paradoxically,

> ... at the same time, that threatens to destroy everything we have, everything we know, everything we are. Modern environments and experiences cut across all boundaries of geography and ethnicity, of class and nationality, of religion and ideology: in this sense, modernity can be said to unite all mankind."[28]

Berman calls this mode of existence and experience "a paradoxical unity, a unity of disunity" and traces it back to a world-order where 'all that is solid melts into air'. In my understanding, modernity ceases to remain a mere

---

[25] For more discussion, refer to Mark Elvin, "A Working Definition of "Modernity"?' in *Past and Present,* no. 113 (November 1986): 209-13.
[26] Marshall Berman, *All that is Solid Melts into Air: The Experiences of Modernity,* (USA, Penguin Books, 1988), 15.
[27] Ibid.
[28] Ibid.

Introduction xxxi

'body of experience' and transcends to become 'experience of body'. I have primarily dealt it as bodily experience or to be more specific as experienced by an ill-body— ill-body as a site of "disintegration and renewal, of struggle and contradiction, of ambiguity and anguish", of alienation and emancipation, of pain and knowledge. And in all these, I have played upon the dialectic of modernism and modernity.

Modernism's relationship with modernity is a double-edged one. The former not only reflects but also reacts against the latter. Modernism is not only a critique but also a critic of the tendencies of modernity. Modernity is a paradigm shift in human thinking and human relations that came about with the advent of modern science, technology, nation-states, money economy, capitalism, and industrialism in the western societies[29]. Thinkers trace the germ of modernity back to René Descartes and his systematic philosophy of looking at things and the kind of disruption it caused to the mind-body suture. Illness, in my thesis, plays the role of a modernist critique as well a critic, and whereby it becomes not only the *symptom* but also the *cure* of modernity.

Søren Kierkegaard likens modernity to 'despair' because it fails to reflect on 'how-to-exist' and, Max Weber likens modernity to 'disenchantment' because of its overabundant emphasis on the quantitative and institutionalised understanding of things. My understanding of illness within the context of modernity, therefore, can be read as both Kierkegaard's 'passion'[30] and Weber's 'enchantment'— illness as my thesis has explained makes one reflect and understand the world around passionately and in an enchanting manner. The *dys-* of the disease is 'passion' (from the Latin *pati* meaning 'to suffer') and is an antidote to technologically propelled 'disenchantment'. In order to exist, we must first learn how to die. As a philosophical tool illness provides a remedy to modernist despair— 'sickness unto death'—that is, not being able to die. Illness in making us learn how-to-die makes us learn how-to-exist. Kierkegaard (although anachronistically) diagnoses the modern predicament and writes:

> When death is the greatest danger, we hope for life; but when we learn to know the even greater danger, we hope for death. When the danger

---

[29] J. Mc Elwee, "The Importance of Philosophy in Human Life", September 17, 2004, http://www.unexplainable.net/info-theories/the importance of philosophy in human life 1882.php (accessed February 2017).
[30] Kierkegaard writes, "[E]xistence, if one becomes conscious of it, involves passion." from Søren Kierkegaard, *Concluding Unscientific Postscript*, ed. Howard V. Hong and Edna H. Hong, (Princeton, Princeton University Press, 1992), 351.

is so great that death becomes the hope, then despair is the hopelessness of not being able to die.[31]

In the wake of the Balkan wars, the two World Wars, the bloody revolutions, the Great Depression, civil wars, the rise of fascism and fascist expansion, Holocaust, atomic rivalry and in many such harrowing experiences, the only remedy that remains is TO DIE. So, the question of understanding how-to-die becomes pivotal to our discussion of modernity and modern age; my select reading of twentieth-century European literature could be identified, therefore, as examples of *ars moriendi*, that is, the art of how-to-die.

Illness cannot be subsumed under the logical order of modernity as it thwarts modernity's project of 'rationalization' and brings into forth a whole new experience of 'being modern'— very different from that of modernity's view of the modern. The figure of an ill individual as withdrawn, reclusive, pensive, and inconsistent resists and subverts the very rubric of the early twentieth-century reason, science and technology. Illness rectifies the Cartesian error which is at the heart of the Enlightenment and concomitantly modernity and reintegrates the once disrupted and ruptured mind-body liaison.

Literature and/as Pathography

So far, I have tried to read Samuel Beckett's *Endgame*, Franz Kafka's select letters, Thomas Mann's *Death in Venice*, Virginia Woolf's *On Being Ill*, and T. S. Eliot's *The Wasteland*— of five different genres—as pathographical accounts and contextualized the same in the discourse of modernity. The texts I have taken are broadly categorized as 'modernist' and do not declare themselves as the sole repository of 'ill', 'illness' or 'ill body'; there are other texts also which are equally, if not more, surcharged with the category of illness. But I have taken into consideration the above mentioned five texts only because they fit into my schemata. I have subjected them to a phenomenological reading and at the end of the day, they somehow explicate and justify what I am trying to put forth here. My process of reading, of unmaking literature, was also to lay bare the making of literature— the way it is made *through* the body and especially, the ill body. The effort here was not only to locate the ill-body-as-it-is-lived in the literary works but also to go beyond and read the *poiesis*— the making of literature— *as* body (herein case, ill body). In my process of remembering illness, something prior but hitherto unnoticed, in relation to the

---

[31] Søren Kierkegaard, *The Sickness Unto Death: A Christian Psychological Exposition of Edification and Awakening by Anti-Climacus*, trans. Alaister Hannay, (UK, Penguin Books, 2004), 18.

Introduction

above mentioned literary works I have tried to 'work through' the pathological disposition of the body.

The role of a pathography is not merely to portray the disturbing experiences of illness and concomitant medical treatment but also to the foreground, at a subjective level, a 'narrative' on incommensurable and inexplicable *angst*. Anne Hunsaker Hawkins points out that, "The medical report is usually composed of brief factual statements about resenting symptoms and body chemistry, whereas a pathography is an extended narrative situating the illness experience within the author's life and the meaning of that life."[32] Pathographical accounts in that sense can be liberating and emancipatory in nature; they reclaim and free the *voices* which were hitherto subdued and ignored under the façade of the medical jargon. A pathography serves as a counter-narrative to the so-called official medical report; the latter does not take into consideration the lived-experience and the lived-body of the sufferer; the former recovers and puts forth the same. The *violence* that is often meted out to the patient's body is justified and, sometimes eulogised in medical case histories. The medical mentality with its repressive medical apparatuses is far from comforting. Modern medical science cures, but it cures without concern. Pathography marks a paradigm shift in the whole medical affair. It rescues the sufferer's point of view from drowning and, by giving voice to it bestows some sort of agency to it. It brings comfort to the already discomforting medical regime. "The task of the author of a pathography", Hunsaker writes, "is not only to describe this disordering process but also to restore to reality its lost coherence and to discover, or create, a meaning that can bind it together again"[33]. Something similar happened in my five chapters. In my *unmaking* of literature, there is a *making* of pathography— in my *making* of pathography, there is an *unmaking* of literature.

My use of illness as a tool of enquiry should strictly be read in relation to the 'somatic turn' that the early twentieth-century took. Before modernity, illnesses were generally associated with spirits, spiritual and moral degradation and many other ecclesiastical and metaphysical speculations. Here I see modernity therefore as a transition from non-corporeality to corporeality— a going back to the body and anything that is, *bodily*. Illness from this perspective then becomes symptomatic of modernity's initial challenge and subsequent subversion of the metaphysics. And what better place to locate those symptoms than to locate them in the twentieth-century European literature! Beckett's drama, Kafka's letters, Mann's fiction, Woolf's memoir and Eliot's

---

[32] Hawkins, *Reconstructing Illness*, 12-13.
[33] Ibid, 2-3.

free verse, then become a hunting ground for modernity, resistance to modernity, literature of the day and philosophy, and the medical suture that ties them up in a reflective and restless bind.

'All this daily drama of pain': Case Studies

Modernity and its contemporary disability find their just representation in the post-Holocaust-like situation of Samuel Beckett's *Endgame*. The first chapter titled 'The Dys-abled Players of Samuel Beckett's *Endgame*' highlights the debilitating conditions of modern existence. The destruction wrought by the two World Wars and the alienation of urban life mingled and created an inhospitable 'human condition' that could only have invented illness— illness not only as a mode of representation but as a state of mind and body. In the Beckettesque reality, bodies are scarcely seen in their corporeality. Rather, bodies become tools for various philosophical and metaphysical speculations. This rupture between reality and corporeality is what makes Beckett an interesting case study for disability studies. Disabled characters and their impaired bodies in the play *Endgame* are also subjected to such hermeneutical speculations. My effort, thus, will be to disembed the hermeneutic continuity and see those bodies in their phenomenological materiality; it would mean going back to the internal structure of pain, suffering and disability.

The lived experience of an impaired body, the body-in-itself, becomes symptomatic of the general human condition in modern times. The incapacity to interact and communicate with the surroundings makes those bodies apprehensive of the inter-subjective and inter-corporeal acknowledgement necessary for survival. The 'restrictive economy' of disability and impairment befalls then into the category of illness as both lived-time and lived-space shrink to the level of *me-here-now*. In the play, we find the two pairs of characters, Hamm-Clov and Nagg-Nell, struggling hard to keep up their spirit alive in the midst of the barrenness of the Absurd stage. Although totally cut-off from the world because of their immobility and blindness, those bodies ironically posit a challenge to the modernist idea of 'speed' and 'movement'. Their illness not only makes them withdraw from the world but also enables them to subvert the rules of the game called *modernity*. Their dys-ability then is not 'meaningless' as conceived by many critics but resists and subverts the form of contemporary disability.

The second chapter titled 'Circumcised Body of Franz Kafka's Select Letters', shall critically investigate Kafka's epistolary conversations which are also in a way his body-writings. Kafka's imagining of his body— an 'overdetermined' body racially and medically infested with different meanings— was a part of the early twentieth-century anti-Semite *weltanschauung*. Such discourses, especially medical discourses were generated to re-produce the Jewish body as abnormal, diseased and deviant— the abject 'other'. It was always a part of his masculinity and racial memory. Tuberculosis the disease he was suffering from, was as much physical as it was psychological, as in one of his letters he points out: "I am mentally handicapped, the lung disease is none other than an overflow of the mental disease"[34]. The 'condemned' body of a Jew, thus, was never far from his mental disposition and vice-versa. This *fin-de-siècle* medicalization and territorialization of the Jewish body, even years after Robert Koch's discovery, add complexities to the entire discourse and paves the way for the construction and dissemination of the Jewish 'imagined body'.

Kafka and his bleeding body with all its flesh and blood and its embodiedness anticipates the condition of the Jewish body during the time of *Shoah*. The racialization and over-medicalization turned the Jewish body into a grotesque body— a body "that defies clear definitions and borders and that occupies the middle ground between life and death, between subject and object, between one and many"[35]. The kind of fluidity that Kafka "deciphers with his wound"[36] can be traced all through his entire oeuvre. The unfinished and ambiguous body of Kafka, suffering from bodily feebleness, somatic otherness, neurasthenia and tuberculosis, signify, as Sander Gilman points out, his existence as a Jewish body. Not only tuberculosis but the very pain and angst of living within the confinements of or rather beyond the boundaries of the societal arrangement lead to the creation of an alien and uncanny self-body. But it was also the same body with all its fleshliness and corporeality that enabled him and those like him to form a non-closed and inter-corporeal subjectivity connected to others in the form of an ethical relationship— the ever unfinished and ever creating body.

The profession of medicine, as Lisa A. Long suggests, sought to objectify the body while the profession of history sought to objectify the past[37]— the circumcised history of the circumcised body. And in this 'somatic turn', Kafka emerges as a brilliant study of the history of the flesh and the history in the flesh, a perfect paradigm of how that demonstrates in the twentieth-century the crises in civilization lead to the crises of representation.

---

[34] Franz Kafka, *Letters to Milena*. trans. Philip Boehm, (New York, Schocken, 1990), 11.
[35] Sara Cohen Shabot, "Grotesque Bodies: A Response to Disembodied Cyborgs" in *Journal of Gender Studies Vol. 16*, no.3, (November 2006): 223-235.
[36] Franz Kafka, Willa Muir and Edwin Muir, *The Penal Colony: Stories and Short Pieces*, (New York, Schocken, Books, 1976), 204.
[37] For more details, please refer Lisa A. Long, *Rehabilitating Bodies: Health, History and the American Civil War*, (Pennsylvania, University of Pennsylvania Press, 2004).

In the third chapter titled 'Connoisseurship... of Disease and Thomas Mann's *Death in Venice*', I deal with one of the most important modern novelists and someone who is often associated with writers like Kafka, Proust and Joyce. Richard Carter points out that Mann was "one of the most medically perceptive writers of this century. He was obsessed with 'connoisseurship of disease', and expressed deep insights and interest in psychosomatic medicine and diverse medical problems"[38]. Such recurrent fascination with sickness and death can be traced throughout his oeuvre: life in a tuberculosis sanatorium in *The Magic Mountain*, cholera epidemic in *Death in Venice*, organ transplantation in *The Transposed Heads*, uterine carcinoma in *The Black Swan*, central nervous syphilis in *Doctor Faustus*. Mann himself claims that all his interest in disease and death is only another expression of interest in life[39].

Mann's *Death in Venice* juxtaposes biological decay, repressed desire and *dépaysement*— the state of being in a foreign, unfamiliar country. In the novella, the beauty of the Venetian city and the destruction of Gustav von Aschenbach's forbidden love for Tadzio are closely interwoven. Set at the backdrop of the cholera epidemic illness becomes a metaphor of a renewed vulnerability to the erotic and the Dionysian impulses ('*Kunsttriebe*'). Von Aschenbach asks himself, "What were art and virtue to him given the advantages of *chaos*?"[40] Playing on the dichotomies of modern life with its divided aims, Mann weaves a narrative based on modern metaphors of illness— illness as metaphors and metaphors as illness. Aschenbach's body, therefore, becomes a site of contestation— an overdetermined body signed by various modern discourses. The stench of morbidity flows like an undercurrent throughout the different modern narratives and Mann's is no different. His treatment of Tadzio, Venice and death are on the same plane. We see the metaphors of illness and death being used over and over again while describing Tadzio and Venice; and the way the modern necropolis of Venice has been portrayed is no different from the morbid Tadzio. Mann diagnoses the fragmentation and decentredness of modern existence and makes an allegory out of it. He also makes an effort to locate the new vision of centre onto illness and death. Mann looks for a cure in illness. Illness in *Death in Venice* then

---

[38] For more details, see Richard Carter, "The Mask of Thomas Mann (1875-1955): Medical Insights and Last Illness" in *The Society of Thoracic Surgeons*, Elsevier Science Inc, no. 65 (1998): 578-585.

[39] Thomas Mann, *The Magic Mountain*, trans. H. T. Lowe Porter, (London, Vintage, 1999), 495.

[40] Thomas Mann, *Death in Venice*, trans. Michael Henry Heim, (New York, Harper Collins, 2004), 125.

Introduction xxxvii

becomes a mode of investigating and exploring the different alternatives of a lost centre. Like the Romantics, Mann regards illness and dying as both an end and a mode of emancipation.

The figure of the recluse generates a threat to the very idea of *modernity*. In the fourth chapter titled 'Undiscovered Countries with Virginia Woolf's *On Being Ill*' I seek to validate the perspective of the invalid and the recluse. In the essay, Woolf traces the journey of a recluse who in illness withdraws from the daily humdrum of life, from the hustle and bustle of the city of health to a room of one's own: a room which allows one to reflect on things around, and see the world both inside and outside in different light. Here, the pre-reflective involvement with the world gives way to a more contemplative and meditative way of looking. Like *epoché*, illness can become a tool for philosophical enquiry. The Romantic empathy of sitting and hearing 'each other groan' is substituted by a modernist disjuncture and 'disinterestedness'. It enables the pensive pathological being to challenge the discourses of modern urban existence driven by machines. The essay captures the adventures of such a being (and its subsequent becoming).

"The best of these illnesses", as Woolf notes in her diary, "is that they loosen the earth about the roots. They make changes. People express their affection" (xviii). Such confessional and yet liberating mode of writing vis-à-vis illness is what constitutes *On Being Ill*— a manifesto of the ideology of illness— first appeared in *New Criterion* in the year 1926. The title alludes to William Hazlitt's 1822 essay *On Going a Journey*. The journey one takes in illness is terrifying, tormenting and agonizing and at the same time, creative and liberating— very symptomatic of the kind of writing Virginia Woolf engages herself into. The genre of 'writing in bed' not only captures the corporeal confinement and spatiotemporal constriction but also in Woolf's case paves the way for a mode of transcendence from *modernity*.

Chapter Five titled 'Connect Nothing with Nothing in T. S. Eliot's *The Wasteland*' (re)reads the most representative poem of the time in which we find a blind transgendered speaker lamenting on the sickness of modern life figured through a king who is suffering from an undiagnosed disease and who fishes by a polluted stream. The speaker encounters a one-eyed merchant, a fortune teller with a bad cold, a clerk with serious acne, and a husband who suffers from nervous disorders ["my nerves are bad tonight" (111)], and listens to the denizens of a pub discuss abortion and the loss of teeth. In the distance, the poem's speaker hears the sound of a young woman who has been raped and whose tongue has been cut out[41]. T. S. Eliot was composing *The Wasteland* (1922) while under the care of Dr. Roger Vittoz at a sanatorium in Switzerland in late 1921 situated on the banks of Lake Léman in Lausanne. Notwithstanding Eliot's famous theory of 'impersonality' and the practice of close reading championed by the New Critics, the biographical (or rather pathographical) account of the poem cannot be overlooked. There cannot be a possible distance between the man who suffers and the mind which creates. The whole intention of the poet was to open the cadaver of the modern society and diagnose the sickness and corruption at its core. The only tragic prognosis that remains then is to "sew him up and let him die in peace"[42].

The Wasteland epitomizes modernism's reaction against modernity. The poem can be read as a pathological narrative— a narrative which diagnoses the problem of alienation, disjuncture, sterility, mechanicality, fragmentation and breakdown of communication and as prognosis prescribes a new vision of centre and a new telos.

My purpose here is to look at certain works of twentieth-century European literature through the prism of illness. And in this play between illness and literature, modernity will serve as a playground. I have treated modernity as a space where I have located not only the experience of illness but also the experiencing-self: not only the suffering, the sufferer too. I have here restricted myself to only an embodied understanding of illness and have not taken into consideration the psychiatric counterpart. I, rather, refuse to see illnesses as only physical or mental. The –ness of ill-ness for me is psychosomatic and beyond; it belongs to the broader realm of lived-body and not restrictive mind or body[43]. Illness is much *more* than just a mind or body or, even mind-body. I have also avoided medical specificities and treated illness as a general category. Although there are passing references to different ailments like cholera, tuberculosis, BDD etcetera, I have not limited my understanding to the modern reductionist and nomothetic understanding of illness, but have gone

---

[41] Michael Davidson, "By the Road to the Contagious Hospital: Invalid Modernism", November 10, 2013, https://www.northumbria.ac.uk/static/.../Lect_4_Fashionable_Diseases.pdf, (accessed January 14, 2017)

[42] T. S. Eliot' s letter to his Mother dated 12 December 1920 in Matthew K. Gold, "The Expert Hand and the Obedient Heart: Dr. Vittox, T.S.Eliot and the Therapeutic Possibilities of The Wasteland", *Journal of Modern Literature XXIII*, no. 3/4 (2000):519-533.

[43] Lived-body, taking a cue from twentieth-century phenomenologists, for me is mind-body and *more than* mind-body. Jean Luc Nancy refers to open body and body *as* open; body as space and spacing at the same time. My understanding of illness, therefore, belongs to and results from such a tradition; free from any such narrow categorisation, illness for me is mind-body and *more than* mind-body.

beyond those diagnostic categories. I am here much more interested in illness *as an* experience rather than illness *as* an event.

Works Cited

Aho, James & Aho, Kevin. *Body Matters: A Phenomenology of Sickness, Disease, and Illness*. Plymouth: Lexington Books, 2008.

Armstrong, Tim. *Modernism, Technology and the Body: A Cultural History*. Cambridge: Cambridge University Press, 1998.

Bakhtin, Mikhail. *Rabelais and His World*. Indianapolis: Indiana Press University, 1965.

Beckett, Samuel. *Endgame & Act Without Words I*. New York: Grove Press, 1957.

Benjamin, Walter. *The Work of Art in the Age of Mechanical Reproduction*. London: Penguin Books Limited, 2008.

Berman, Marshall. *All that is Solid Melts into Air: The Experiences of Modernity*. USA: Penguin Books, 1988.

Carter, Richard. 'The Mask of Thomas Mann (1875-1955): Medical Insights and Last Illness'. The Society of Thoracic Surgeons, Elsevier Science Inc, 1998.

Charon, Rita. *Narrative Medicine: Honoring the Stories of Illness*. New York: Oxford University Press. 2006.

Charon, Rita. 'Narrative Medicine: A Model for Empathy, Reflection, Profession, and Trust'. *JAMA*. October 17, 2001—Vol. 286.No. 15.1897-1902.

Clewell, Tammy. *Modernism and Nostalgia: Bodies, Locations, Aesthetics*. New York: Palgrave Macmillan. 1993.

Crawford, T. Hugh. *Modernism, Medicine, and William Carlos Williams*. Norman: University of Oklahoma Press, 1993.

Davidson, Michael. 'By the Road to the Contagious Hospital: Invalid Modernism'. https://www.northumbria.ac.uk/static/.../Lect_4_Fashionable_Diseases.pdf (November 10, 2013)

Eliot, T. S. Eliot. *The Complete Poems and Plays of T. S. Eliot*. London: Faber & Faber, 1969.

Elvin, Mark. "A Working Definition of 'Modernity'?" *Past & Present*, no. 113, 1986, pp. 209–213., www.jstor.org/stable/650986.

Foucault, Michel. *The Birth of the Clinic*. London: Routledge, 1997.

Frank, Arthur W. *The Wounded Storyteller: Body, Illness, and Ethics*. Chicago: The University of Chicago Press, 1995.

Gadamer, Hans-Georg. *The Enigma of Health: The Art of Healing in a Scientific Age*. California: Stanford University Press, 1996.

Gilman, Sander. *Franz Kafka, the Jewish Patient*. London: Routledge, 1995.

Gold, Mathew K. 'The Expert Hand and the Obedient Heart: Dr.Vittoz, T. S. Eliot, and the Therapeutic Possibilities of *The Wasteland*'. *Journal of Modern Literature*, XXIII, 3-4 (Summer 200). Indianapolis: Indiana Press University. 2001. 519-533.

Hawkins, Anne Hunsaker. *Reconstructing Illness: Studies in Illness*. Indiana: Purdue University Press, 1999.

Kafka, Franz. *Letters to Friends, Family, and Editors*, Ed. Max Brod.Trans. James stern and Elisabeth Duckworth.New York: Schocken, 1977.

Kafka, Franz., Muir, E., and Muir, W. *The Penal Colony, Stories and Short Pieces.* New York: Schocken Books, 1976.

Kafka, Franz. *Letters to Milena.* Trans. Philip Boehm.New York: Schocken, 1990.

Kierkegaard, Søren. *Concluding Unscientific Postscript.*Trans. Alastair Hannay. Cambridge: Cambridge University Press, 2009.

Kierkegaard, Søren. *The Sickness unto Death: A Christian Psychological Exposition of Edification and Awakening by Anti-Climacus.* Trans. Alastair Hannay. UK: Penguin Books. 2004.

Klienman, Arthur. *The Illness Narrative: Suffering, Healing and the Human Condition.* The US: Basic Books, 1988.

Leder, Drew. *The Absent Body.* Chicago: The University Press of Chicago, 1990.

Levin, David M. 'Mudra as Thinking: Developing Our Wisdom-of-Being in Gestures and Movements' in Parkes. Graham. *Heidegger and Asian Thought.* Delhi: MotilalBanarsidas Publishers, 2010. 245-270.

Long, Lisa A. *Rehabilitating Bodies: Health, History and the American Civil War.*Pennsylvania: University of Pennsylvania, 2004.

Mann, Thomas. *The Magic Mountain*, Trans. H. T. Lowe Porter. London: Vintage, 1999.

Mann, Thomas. *Death in Venice.*Trans. Michael Henry Heim. New York: Harper Collins, 2004.

McEntyre, Marilyn Chandler. *Patient Poets: Illness from Inside Out.*San Francisco: University of California Medical Humanities Press, 2012.

Merleau-Ponty, Maurice. *The Phenomenology of Perception.* Trans. C. Smith.New Jersey: Humanities Press, 1962.

Nancy, Jean Luc. *Being Singular Plural.*Trans. Robert D. Richardson and Anne E. O'Byrne. Stanford: Stanford University Press, 2000.

Nancy, Jean-Luc.*Corpus.*Trans. Richard Rand.New York: Fordham University Press, 2008.

Quayson, Ato. *Aesthetic Nervousness: Disability and the Crisis of Representation.*New York: Columbia University Press, 2007.

Sartre, Jean Paul. *Being and Nothingness: An Essay on Phenomenological Ontology.* Trans. Hazel E. Barnes.London: Routledge, 1958.

Scarry, Elaine.*The Body in Pain: The Making and Unmaking of the World.* Oxford: Oxford University Press, 1985.

Slattery, Dennis Patrick. *The Wounded Body: Remembering the Markings of Flesh.* New York: State University of New York Press, 2000.

Sontag, Susan. *Illness as Metaphor,* New York: Vintage Books, 1978.

Toombs, S. K. *The Meaning of Illness: A Phenomenological Account of the Different Perspectives of Physician and Patient.*Boston: Kluwer Academic Pub, 1992.

Weber, Max. *The Protestant Ethic and the Spirit of Capitalism.* New York: Dover Publications, 2012.

Woolf, Virginia & Stephen, Julia.*On Being Ill* with *Notes from Sick Rooms.* Massachusetts: Paris Press, 2012.

Chapter 1

The Dys-abled Players of Samuel Beckett's *Endgame*

> I say to myself— sometimes, Clov you must learn to suffer *better* than that if you want them to weary of punishing you— one day.
>
> Clov in Beckett's *Endgame*

Beckett's corpus abounds in maimed bodies, disabled bodies, incarcerated bodies, grotesque bodies, painful bodies— bodies even though in crisis are never seen in their phenomenological materiality. Rather, those bodies become a cradle for different philosophical and metaphysical speculations. These are always already de-contextualised and de-animated and are free from the socio-political condition and the spiritual and organic semblances. These become what Foucault has called, 'military machine' (*machine á guerir*), "not as a self-healing whole, but as an object, a hindrance to be mastered and made-over design"[1]. The singularity and specificity of the body is completely ignored for the sake of some already established categories and, "[t]hus" as Ato Quayson points out "discussions of maimed and disabled characters in Beckett are often conducted around two broad rubrics: existential phenomenology and deconstructive antihumanism"[2]. In Beckett, there always remains a rupture between disability and pain.

Beckett himself suffered from various chronic ailments including arrhythmic heartbeat, cysts and abscesses and hence, it is no surprise that his *weltanschauung* is layered with different metaphors of illness. Deirdre Bair in *Samuel Beckett: A Biography* points out that "at one point Beckett insisted that all of life was a disease, with babyhood its beginning. Man, to him, was the prime example of the mortally ill, for man began as a helpless infant, unable to attend to himself, and most of the time ended in the same manner. In man's beginning and end, there was immobility, and each man was thus at

---

[1] Aho and Aho, *Body Matters*, 146.
[2] Ato Quayson, *Aesthetic Nervousness: Disability and the Crisis of Representation*, (New York, Columbia University Press, 2007), 56.

the mercy of all others"[3]. Beckett's dereliction for human and humanity makes him employ illness and disability as chimerical devices in his works. There is no distinction between human and the other in Beckett. In him we find a journey from the anthropological to the non-anthropological— in Beckett, the human is the *other* to the extent that it is discontinuous and deformed.[4]

Disease, decay, deterioration and dismemberment are the archetypes we find in profusion in Beckett's plays and novels, but they are seldom associated with physical suffering. They are, rather, often conceived as allegorical— in many cases as symptoms of spiritual and creative debasement. This obliterates the very specificity of the body and the body-in-pain, succumbing to what Quayson calls the "hermeneutical conundrum"— "not so much so as to raise doubt about what it might mean, but so that the entire apparatus of representation is riddled with gaps and aporias"[5]. The play *Endgame* is filled with gaps and aporias or what Theodor Adorno calls 'organized meaninglessness' and 'an expression of meaning's absence'[6]. The disabled and the impaired bodies in the play thus, concomitantly, are never seen in their physiological and phenomenological realities; the studies on Beckettian dramaturgy are more centred around the body as an idea or an ideal.

The play dramatizes the disability of two pairs of characters: Hamm and Clov on one hand and Nagg and Nell on the other. But all these four characters have been tied together in such a manner that it would be almost impossible for a character to live autonomously and might perish in no time if taken out of this arrangement. Hamm is completely blind, crippled and immobile and his entire existence is contingent upon Clov. He will die in no time if Clov leaves him. On the other hand, Clov is mobile and healthier. He is the only character who can move from one corner of the stage to another. He always threatens to leave Hamm but never does ["I'll leave you, I have things to do" (15)]. He is aligned to Hamm because of some unknown reasons. In the case of Nagg and Nell, we see a sort of radical captivation— they are both physical-

---

[3] Beckett used to suffer from various ailments and which in a way influenced his writing, for more details see Deidre Bair, *Samuel Beckett: A Biography*, (New York: Touchstone, 1993), 170.

[4] Paul Sheehan, *Modernism, Narrative and Humanism*, (New York, Oxford University Press, 2004), 176.

[5] Ibid, 84-5.

[6] Theodore Adorno, "Trying to Understand Endgame", *New German Critique*, no.26, (Spring-Summer 1982): 119-150. It has been quoted from Theodore Adorno, "Trying to Understand Endgame" in *Samuel Beckett: Longman Critical Reader*, eds. Jennifer Birkett and Kate Ince, (Essex, Pearson Education, 1999), 41-42.

ly and psychologically confined in their ash cans, totally cut-off from the world as well as from each other. The absurdity of the situation is thus, very striking. In the play, Clov's movement is in sharp contrast to the stillness of Hamm, Nagg and Nell. Quayson observes further that, "the dialectical relationship between mobility and immobility in a play constituted exclusively by characters that carry impairments serves to further accentuate the existential constraint of disability. Every move within this dialectic is constitutively dependent on its opposite, thus suggesting that impairment/disability/immobility and nondisability/mobility are part of a single continuum"[7]. Such radical interdependency becomes necessary especially when one is encountering a post-Holocaust-like situation:

Hamm: [...]
Why do you stay with me?

Clov: Why do you keep me?

Hamm: There's no one else.

Clov: There's nowhere else.

[*Pause.*] (13)

Moreover, Hamm's physical incapacity on the stage has been placed in striking contrast to Clov's mental incapacity that disables him to go from the stage and away from Hamm. Being completely blind and immobile Hamm does not have any direct control over Clov, but we still see him exerting some sort of *indirect* control over Clov and Clov's subsequent internalization of Hamm's authority. It is this internalization which helps in his confinement— when other's gaze is internalized it creates a stand-still, arresting one's essential 'becoming'; it binds it to the 'me-here-now'. This objectification captivates one's self and initiates the process of extermination of one's subjectivity. And here Victoria Swanson draws a parallel between Sartre and Beckett and points out that, "[t]he organizing consciousness, the consciousness of the observer, displaces and objectifies the subject. Sartre and Beckett both present the gaze of the 'Other' as violent and subjectifying"[8]. But, as opposed to Sartre, there is

---

[7] Quayson, *Aesthetic Nervousness*, 68.
[8] Victoria Swanson, "Confining, Incapacitating, and Partitioning the Body: Carcerality and Surveillance in Samuel Beckett's *Endgame, Happy Days*, and *Play*", *Miranda*, no.4, http://miranda.revues.org/, (October 25, 2011), 2.

no provision for freedom, will and authenticity in Beckettesque reality. Rather, she argues that "Beckett embraces the impossibility of meaning as liberation from confinement inherent with predicaments of subjectivity, power, and the limitations of language"[9]. She points out that "[f]or Beckett, the Sartrean vision of subjectivity is a trap that can only be escaped, if it can at all, by the kind of self-violence that leads to self-dissolution"[10], something that can be seen in Clov's subjectivation and subjugation by Hamm:

> **Clov:** I can't sit down.
>
> **Hamm:** [*impatiently*] Well you will lie down then, what the hell! Or you'll come to a standstill, simply stop and stand still, the way you are now. One day you'll say, I am tired, I'll stop. What does the attitude matter?
>
> [*Pause*]
>
> **Clov:** So you all want me to leave you.
>
> **Hamm:** Naturally.
>
> **Clov:** Then I'll leave you.
>
> **Hamm:** You can't leave us.
>
> **Clov:** Then I won't leave you.
>
> [*Pause*] (44-45)

So, vulnerability in the play not only comes from corporeal confinement but psychological confinement also. Both Hamm and Clov are confined to the stage in their own way— the former because of his physical impairment and, the latter because of his subjectivity and carcerality. It is only through his chaotic function, through his "repeated violations" that Clov will be able to disrupt this very power relation and "transform the abode into a pandemonium"[11].

---

[9] Ibid, 3.
[10] Ibid.
[11] Samuel Beckett, "The Lost Ones", *The Complete Short Prose 1929-1989*, (New York, Grove Press, 1995) 209.

All the four characters in the play including Clov are incapacitated—they are at disease with the world (though it will be very difficult for me to use the words 'disease' and 'disability' interchangeably). Their lack of ability (read, disability) to interact with the other creates a rupture between their being and the world. Similarly, our bodies too live in relation to the other. Our bodies act as a bridge between the "self" and the "world"— the world is not 'out there' separated from our being but a situation which can easily be deemed as body-in-the-world and body-with-the-world. It is always already embedded, enmeshed, entangled with the world. So what the characters in the play lack is the inter-subjective acknowledgement; they remain not only physiologically but ontologically fractured, bruised, alienated and paranoid. Their incapacity to interact and communicate with the surrounding makes them a deficit of the state of 'holiness'— the wholeness, completeness, balance which we call 'health'. They are all apprehensive and paranoid about their surroundings, abiding by the Sartrean thesis "Hell is— other people"[12]. It is this cynicism that is disabling them to escape from their situation— they are all either incarcerated or self-incarcerated:

Hamm: Outside of here it's death.

[*Pause*] (16)

And again,

Hamm: Stop!

[*Clov stops chair close to back wall. Hamm lays his hand against wall.*]

Old wall!

Beyond is the...other hell.

[*Pause. Violently.*]

Closure! Closure! Up against! (33)

---

[12] For strong points of view on the issue, see Jean Paul-Sartre, *No Exit and The Time Flies* (New York, Knopf, 1946), 61.

Thus, all the players in Beckett's play are restricted to their limited time and space— Hamm to his wheel-chair, Nagg and Nell to their ash cans and Clov to the stage. The shrinking of time and space is one of the highlights of *Endgame*. The 'restrictive economy' of Beckettian stage does not provide any scope for transcendence.

The lived space, the familiar territory of the characters in the play shrinks as their impairments are turned into disabilities. Their bodies no more stretched 'ex-statically' into lived space; rather, we see restricted bodily functions and contraction of space. Their bodies lack what Maurice Merleau-Ponty would call *praktognosia* or kinesthetic wisdom. James Aho and Kevin Aho explain how during the period one is healthy, the "body stretches 'ex-statically' into lived space, beyond the limits of my skin" and how during illness this ability, the ability of 'I can' changes into the inability of 'I can't'[13]. In illness, they write:

> the world no longer gives itself as an expansive horizon of possibilities into which I can pass. Instead, the stairs look *insurmountable*, the door is *too heavy*, and sitting is *painful*. The boundaries of my world begin to collapse"[14].

Such bodily restrictions and 'freezing and rigidity of the lived-body' accentuate disability and immobility as one is pinned down to a particular space and never move and act beyond the *vicinity*. The players refuse leaving their *vicinity* since all that they can be sure of is their *vicinity*, nothing further than the vicinity:

Hamm: Nature has forgotten us.

Clov: There is no more nature.

Hamm: No more nature? You exaggerate.

Clov: In the *vicinity*. (18)

The actions in the play are very much restricted as there is no intersubjectivity, no intercorporeality, no 'bodying-forth'— we see a contraction of both lived-body and lived-space. The bodies in the play fail to transcend their skin, their *körper*, they remain always already limited to their corporeality; and any attempt to establish a relationship with the world remains futile. Hamm,

---

[13] For a more detailed discussion on the subject, see Aho and Aho, *Body Matters*, 115-7.
[14] Ibid.

Nagg, Nell and, to a certain extent Clov stay caged in their machine-like bodies and become what La Mettrie has called *l'homme machine*, that is devoid of any of the essential 'becoming(s)'. None of the characters enjoy what they do. And as space is 'narrowing' upon them, their life is being reduced to its bare minimum (or, 'bare life'). We witness such claustrophobic ambience in the very stagecraft and such 'narrowing' down since the beginning of the play:

Bare interior.

Grey light.

Left and right back, high up, two small windows, curtains drawn. Front right, a door. Hanging near door, its face to wall, a picture. Front left, touching each other, covered with an old sheet, two ashbins. Center, in an armchair on castors, covered with an old sheet, Hamm. Motionless by the door, his eyes fixed on Hamm, Clov. Very red face. Brief tableau. (7)

It is all that Beckettian stage has to offer: life reduced to its bare minimum. The 'bare interior' and closed spaces of the stage are symptomatic of not only the nadir of life but also a shrinking of lived-space resulting from impairment and disability. "That is to say, there is a narrowing or 'funneling' of our existence down to essentials. Life close in on us; we stop doing things that once nourished and nourished us, leaving only work or other stressors that continue to deplete our emotional resources. The narrower the funnel becomes, the easier it is to be drawn into the hallowed-out state of having but one choice, either to live or die"[15]. Disability and space are, thus, directly proportional to each other.

Not only do we see shrinkage of lived space in *Endgame* but also shrinkage of lived-time—the continuum of time which anticipates what-is-to-come (the future) relative to what-is- now (the present) and to what-once-was (the past). The temporal existence of the characters on stage is reduced to their immediacy as if they are stuck or glued to their present "now". They have become prisoners of the present and confined to their single temporal dimension. Unsure about their past their future seem to be very dark and bleak. In illness, "the lived past", as James and Kevin Aho point out, "with its remembered images of vitality and independence closes off. The remaining memories are stripped of their emotional valence and begin showing up in an alien and abstract way as the experiences of someone else" and on the other hand

---

[15] See Williams, Teasdale, Segal and Kabat-Zinn, *The Mindful Way through Depression*, 28-29. It has been quoted from Aho and Aho, *Body Matters*, 120.

"once open vista of future hopes and dreams collapses"[16]. The illness and impairment in the play cause the rhythmic flow of time to stop and shrink, disabling them to think and act beyond the limits of the stage time. So not only *here* but 'outside of *now* its death' as well.

In the play, we do not find any of the characters transcending the limits of the time on stage. "Nothing seems to happen in the now of the dramatic action. All that is left for the characters is the recollection of the past"[17], as Quayson points out. We see Hamm, and especially, Nagg and Nell taking recourse to the past as a respite from the pain of the present—dreariness and weariness of their present existence:

Hamm: I love the *old* questions.

[*With fervor*]

Ah the *old* questions, the *old* answers, there's nothing like them!

[…] (46)

Although their effort to (re)create the past in order to suit their present proves futile, it provides them some kind of anesthesia — momentary relief from their painful sterile condition. Nagg and Nell remain isolated from each other in their separate ash bins. They do not share anything in the 'here, now' of the stage but that lack of '-with-the-other' is compensated by a shared past. They were hardly able to see each other, but they could hear properly and it was their narrative (of the past) that was keeping them alive:

Nagg: Can you see me?

Nell: Hardly. And you?

Nagg: What?

Nell: Can you see me?

Nagg: Hardly.

---

[16] See Aho and Aho, *Body Matters*, 120-121.
[17] Quayson, *Aesthetic Nervousness*, 68.

Nell: So much the better, so much the better.

Nagg: Don't say that.

[*Pause.*]

Our sight has failed.

Nell: Yes

[*Pause. They turn away from each other.*]

Nagg: Can you hear me?

Nell: Yes. And you?

Nagg: Yes.

[*Pause.*]

Our hearing hasn't failed. [...]

Nagg: Do you *remember*—

[...] (22)

The narrative of what had happened on Lake Como in this particular scene juxtaposes the past with the present or to be more correct, the *ability* of the past with the *disability* of the present. So for Nagg and Nell, "the process of recalling the past is at the same time a process of animating what is potentially sterile and inert, that is, dead and only enlivened in memory"[18]. Such interlocutions help to build up the conflict— mnemonic interludes of *action* in the play exist in stark contrast to the general *inaction* on the stage.

The experience of pain and disability remains unaccounted throughout the play. Although in pain none of the characters recognize it. Only in a few instances, we find Hamm asking for painkillers; but, pain and, especially physical pain, remains unrecognized and uncertain. We do not see any articulation of the body in pain, of the body which is suffering— a condition which can be

---

[18] Ibid, 71.

called *painfulness without pain* where one is able to be in pain but is not able to feel pain. Such ambiguous and perplexed status of pain in the play is the consequence of the contradiction between *being in pain* and *feeling pain*. Pain is always already contingent upon intersubjective recognition— the validation of pain of the sufferer is somewhat validated by the recognition of the other. In *Body in Pain* (1985), Elaine Scarry suggests that one of the complex things about pain is that it produces epistemological certainty for the pain sufferer but the possibility of doubt for the nonsufferer. "To have pain," Scarry points out, "is to have *certainty*; to hear about pain is to have *doubt*"[19]. There is no 'analogical verification' or 'analogical substantiation', to draw Scarry again, of pain in Beckett's plays. *Endgame* employs a whole new structure of interlocution by disrupting and reframing the very relationship between the sufferer and the witness. There is no recognition and there is no effort on the part of the characters to alleviate pain: they remain indifferent to each other's pain. Hamm's demand for painkillers is never meted out by Clov. Hamm, on the other hand, never takes Clov's pain seriously. And they both stay oblivious to the hunger, pain and suffering of Nagg and Nell:

Hamm: [...]

Is it not time for my pain killers?

Clov: No

[*Pause.*]

I'll leave you, I have things to do. (14)

And again,

Hamm: How are your eyes?

Clov: Bad

Hamm: How are your legs?

Clov: Bad

---

[19] For strong points of view on different aspects of the issue, see Scarry, *Body in Pain*, 4.

Hamm: But you can move.

Clov: Yes.

Hamm: [*violently*] Then move! (14)

Quayson points out, "[t]he absence of a structure of interlocution for addressing pain in Beckett is what allows his drama, in particular, to reside uneasily between tragedy and comedy. The dianoetic laughter that often attends plays such as *Endgame* is possible because the characters' suffering is not physical or even indeed emotional. They are not perceived to be in pain in any physical sense of the word"[20]. Rather than evoking pathos, the situation of the characters tends to evoke bathos. The characters in the play are often thought to be ciphers and their act nothing more than clowning. Nell diagnoses the problem and critiques their situation, as he says:

Nell: One mustn't laugh at those things, Nagg. Why must you always laugh at them?

Nagg: Not so loud!

Nell: [without lowering her voice] Nothing is funnier than unhappiness. I grant you that... (26)

The negation of any real referent of physical pain and discomfort firstly, from the stage, secondly, from the structure of impairment and disability, thirdly, from the minds of the characters and, fourthly, the relationship between them enable the play to fall victim to several metaphysical categories or speculations. In order to understand the Beckettesque world, the *anamnēsis* of the sheer complexities surrounding pain and suffering is required. In his reading of the play, Ranjan Ghosh refers to these phenomena and succinctly raises some fundamental questions centering on the idea of suffering and the very (non)experience of suffering: "affecting the life of the self, the spirit, and the body" not only in the play but also the life outside[21]. He questions:

---

[20] See Quayson, *Aesthetic Nervousness*, 83.
[21] Ranjan Ghosh, "Reading and Experiencing a Play Transculturally", *Comparative Drama Vol. 46, no.3* (2012): 260-281.

Why is this suffering, and what is the suffering for? [...] Does *Endgame* provide us with a means by which to judge the reality and vitality of suffering? How do we account for such a dismembered and disjointed world?[22]

The 'overdetermination' of suffering and physical pain can be observed throughout the play. Even the three-legged castrated dog that Clov uses in the play to hit Hamm can be seen as an allusion to Friedrich Nietzsche's metaphor for pain. In *The Gay Science* Nietzsche writes: "I have given a name to my pain and call it 'dog'. It is just as faithful, just as obtrusive and shameless, just as entertaining, just as clever as any other dog— and I can scold it and vent my bad mood on it, as others do with their dogs, servants, and wives."[23] Perhaps, even Clov himself can be seen as a reification of Hamm's unbearable pain. He never gives Hamm his painkillers. The entire existence of Hamm is conditional and depends on Clov heavily. The latter, on the other hand, always threatens Hamm but never leaves ("I'll leave you, I have things to do"). They equally surmount Hamm— *like* pain, *like* Clov. The pain is more of a cipher in Beckettesque reality making it very difficult to read. The disabled and impaired bodies in *Endgame* and the "precise metacritical function" that they serve to make them elusive and ambiguous in nature rendering the "entire apparatus of representation... riddled with gaps and aporia"[24].

Beckett's plays diagnose the limits of lived body. In *Theatre and Body*, Colette Conroy points out, "the body" for Beckett "is a metaphor for the restrictive experiences of the human psyche and its failure to escape from its own painful restrictions"[25]. There is no 'escape' in Beckett's theatre and in *Endgame*, the uncanny immobility on the stage never allows any extant for freedom and transcendence. Although in the play we find Hamm once hinting at such an escape to a distant land, "Let's go from *here*, the two of us! South! You can make a raft and the currents will carry us, far away, to other... mammals!" (42) but very soon his *anagnorisis* of pain brings him down to his bodily existence: "Wait! [...] Is it not yet time for my pain-killer?" The limits of 'here, now' of the stage *limit* the agency of the characters— not allowing them to come out of their 'restrictive economy' of corporeal existence.

The lived body becomes a tool to study different dimensions of disability in theatre. Conroy claims "[t]here is a huge difference between talking about 'the

---

[22] Ibid.
[23] See Nietzsche, *The Gay Science*, trans. Walter Kaufmann, (New York, Vintage, 1974), 249.
[24] See Quayson, *Aesthetic Nervouness*, 83.
[25] Colette Conroy, *Theatre and the Body*, (New York, Palgrave Macmillan, 2010), 73.

body' and its experience of a theatre performance and talking about 'bodies' and their experiences. 'The body' supposes that there is an ideal or assumed body and that all people gain access to the pleasures of performance in broadly the same way. When we think about *bodies* as entities that see, feel and move in radically different ways, as in disability theatre, the idealized *body* becomes the disparate *bodies*. We can't suppose that the play offers one overriding 'meaning' or a single coherent performance."[26] The (re)presentation of disability and impairment in Beckett's *Endgame* blast open the very continuum of hermeneutics, challenging the 'ideal' and calling for an array of possibilities. There is no end to this game. By continuously resisting and subverting the notions of the body, pain, disability and action Beckett is trying to change the very rules of the game. The body, pain, illness and impairment in the play are not what we understand off-stage. On-stage the exceptional bodies of Hamm, Clov, Nagg, and Nell incite violence, encourage representation and persistently force explanation. They managed to suffer *better* even when sufferance was looming large. The play rather becomes a game to end the kind of conventional politics prevalent both on and off the stage.

Works Cited

Aho, James & Aho, Kevin. *Body Matters: A Phenomenology of Sickness, Disease, and Illness*. Plymouth, UK: Lexington Books, 2008.

Bair, Deidre. *Samuel Beckett: A Biography*. New York: Touchstone, 1993.

Beckett, Samuel. *Endgame & Act Without Words I*. New York: Grove Press, 1957.

Beckett, Samuel. "The Lost Ones". The Complete Short Prose, 1929-1989. New York: Grove Press, 1995.

Conroy, Colette. *Theatre and the Body*. New York: Palgrave Macmillan, 2010.

Ghosh, Ranjan. 'Reading and Experiencing a Play Transculturally'. *Comparative Drama Vol. 45 No. 3*. Michigan: Western Michigan University, 2012. 260-281.

Nietzsche, Friedrich. *The Gay Science*.trans. Walter Kaufmann. New York: Vintage,1974.

Quayson, Ato. *Aesthetic Nervousness: Disability and Crisis of Representation*. New York: Columbia University Press, 2007.

Sartre, Jean-Paul.*No Exit and The Flies*. New York: Knopf, 1946.

Scarry, Elaine.*The Body in Pain: The Making and Unmaking of the World*. Oxford and New York: Oxford University Press, 1985.

Sheehan, Paul. *Modernism, Narrative and Humanism*. UK: Cambridge University Press. 2004.

---

[26] For further discussion, see ibid, 55-6.

Swanson, Victoria. Confining, Incapacitating, and Partitioning the Body: Carcerality and Surveillance in Samuel Beckett's *Endgame, Happy Days*, and *Play*. in Miranda [Online]. Université Toulouse. http://miranda.revues.org/. 2011.

Williams, M. J. Teasdale, Z. Segal, and J. Kabat-Zinn. *The Mindful Way through Depression: Freeing Yourself from Chronic Unhappiness*. New York: The Guilford Press, 2007.

Chapter 2

The Circumcised Body of Franz Kafka's Select Letters

I am constantly trying to communicate something *incommunicable*, to explain something *inexplicable*, to tell about something I only feel in my bones and which can only be experienced in those bones.

-Kafka, *Letters to Milena*

One is not born a Jew but becomes one. The becomings and micro-becomings in Kafka are symptomatic of a process of destabilization: his (micro)struggle against the agencies of the day. The struggle is between coming out of his Jewishness and, at the same time, to assert and maintain the Jewishness with all its differences and multiplicities. The destratification and fluidity of Kafka's poetics is not very uncomplicated, but its ambiguity lies in the fact that the process of becoming-Jew involves destabilizing the molar Jewish identity as well as creating a new one while preserving the old. If one is a Jew, then it becomes very important to maintain that Jewishness. *That* Jewishness, nevertheless, is nothing but a Deleuzian "empty body-without-organ" (BwO), unable to connect with other bodies, an existence inward, cut off from the rest of the world— the kind of alienation and loneliness that one finds in his oeuvre[1]. In Kafka, we find a being severing all ties with the world, a narrative becoming notes from the underground and a voice more of a victim of the hidden structures of subjectivity which one can neither escape nor understand. His epistles are not an exception: his epistolary conversations with Max Brod, Felice Bauer, Milena Jesenská, and Hermann Kafka become then a brilliant case study of Kafka's tryst with the *enigmatic* tuberculosis. The disease retained its romantic notion even in the first half of the twentieth century. Susan Sontag points out how even after the decline in a number of

---

[1] For detailed discussion on the subject, see Gilles Deleuze and Felix Guattari, *A Thousand Plateaus: Capitalism and Schizophrenia*, trans. B. Masumi, (Minneapolis, University of Minnesota Press, 1987) and Gilles Deleuze and Felix Guattari, *Anti-Oedipus: Capitalism and Schizophrenia*, trans. R. Hurley, M. Seem and H. R. Lane, (Minneapolis, University of Minnesota Press, 1983).

cases in the twentieth century, the disease retained its mysterious and edifying nature. The incidences of TB, as Sontag points out,

> ... began to decline precipitously after 1900 because of improved hygiene, the mortality rate among those who contracted it remained high; the power of the myth was dispelled only when proper treatment was finally developed, with the discovery of streptomycin in 1944 and the introduction of isoniazid in 1952.[2]

The shame, guilt, stigma and the concomitant alienation are results of not only his Jewishness but of his pathological condition also, to the extent that his Jewishness was never free from his illness. His subjectivity and his poetics were always already dictated by his pathology so much so that his 'I am' was never really far from 'I am sick'. This ontico-ontology of 'I am, therefore I am sick' and 'I am sick therefore I am' made him to think of himself as a 'foreign body' cut off from the life-world. This non-human, stigmatized, diseased and fragmented body lacks any kind of agency— a body which can be observed, grasped and manipulated at will, a body ruthlessly exposed to the other, an object, a 'body-for-other' (*corps pour autrui*).

The binary between 'I am' and 'I am sick', between health and illness, gets a whole new expression in the form of military images. The metaphor of battle used for any diseased body is commonplace in various pathographical accounts. The idea of conflict between a normal self and a violent pathological non-self is something that takes us away from the body itself to a world of metaphors and symbols. Even Kafka uses such expressions to communicate something which is *incommunicable* and to explain something which is *inexplicable*, as he writes to his fiancée Felice Bauer referring to this fight:

> For secretly I don't believe this illness to be tuberculosis, at least not primarily tuberculosis, but rather a sign of my general bankruptcy. I had thought the war could last longer, but it can't. The blood issues not from the lung, but from a decisive stab delivered by one of the combatants.
>
> [...] Simply because it is not the kind of tuberculosis that can be laid in a deck chair and nursed back to health, but a weapon that continues to be of supreme necessity as long as I remain alive. And both cannot remain alive.[3]

---

[2] Susan Sontag, *Illness as Metaphor*, (New York: Vintage Books, 1978), 34.
[3] Franz Kafka, *Letters to Felice*, ed. Erich Heller and Jurgen Born, (New York, Schocken, 1982), 545-46.

The 'general bankruptcy' of which Kafka talks about is as much socio-political as personal and considers tuberculosis a mere manifestation of that. The metaphor of war stands for his constant struggle against the status quo of the period as well as his own body. He considers the latter a 'major obstacle'. He considers himself as much a victim of contemporary politics as his own ill body— both brought an equal amount of shame, guilt and dejection to Kafka; both objectified and corporealized Kafka in equal terms. Kafka's notion of his own body can be compared with that of someone suffering from Body Dysmorphic Disorder (BDD) or body-image disorder, a form of obsessive self-loathing with regard to one's own body or any of its parts. In the case of Kafka, it was both the result of his Jewishness and illness. The *otherisation* of his own body is reflected in the following lines from a never-sent-letter to his father:

> Since there was nothing at all I was certain of, since I needed to be provided at every instant with a new confirmation of my existence, since nothing was in my very own, undoubted, sole possession, determined unequivocally only by me — in sober truth a disinherited son — naturally I became unsure even of the thing nearest to me, my own body.[4]

A sound subject body's gaze is projected towards the other, towards the world; the other remains the centre of a gaze. But the moment the world starts to look at the self, the self becomes the centre of a gaze and starts looking inward rather than outward, reflecting on the body as an object. This objectification or corporealization captivates one's self and initiates the process of extermination of one's subjectivity. Such kind of reductionism is a threat to the self, its agency and its spontaneity. This event of desubjectivation, striping someone of all its vitalities, occurred at many levels for the Jewish body. The Jewish body and its nakedness were exposed in public areas making it a site of ridicule, anger and utter abjection; it is often compared to that of the sewage system, the channel of expulsion where people could vent out their spleen. Words like "ventilating, evacuating, circulating, deodorizing, regulating, managing, draining, cleansing, privatizing", used by Alain Corbin[5] while talking about modern sewage system, was also a part of anti-Semite *Weltanschauung* and was used as a linguistic detox. This was in a way very important in the process of maintaining the psychological and social hygiene of the

---

[4] Franz Kafka, "Letters to the Father", *The Sons*, trans. Ernst Kaiser and Eithne Wilkens, (New York, Schocken, 1989).
[5] A. Corbin, *The Foul and the Fragrant: Odor and the French Social Imagination*, (Cambridge, Harvard University Press, 1986), 102.

Volkskorper. Kafka writes to Milena on 26 August 1920: "I am dirty, Milena, infinitely dirty, this is why I scream so much about purity."[6]

When the scrutinizing gaze of the other is internalized, the body-for-itself gives way to the body-for-other, creating a stand-still which tends to arrest body's essential 'becoming' and binds it to 'me-here-now': a condition that corporealizes the pre-reflective lived-body (*leib*). The pre-reflective body and the corporeal body (*korper*) do not exist in the manner of Cartesian duality but are dialectically intertwined always. It presents itself as a way of being-in-the-world, that is, the lived-body (*leib*). In illness this pre-reflective body which was hitherto absent foregrounds itself violently disrupting the very harmony of with-the-other. The concord of existence is replaced by the discord of existence: body becomes an *obstacle* the moment it becomes diseased. Kafka writes in one of his diary entries about this body-image disorder:

> It is certain that a major *obstacle* to my progress is my physical condition. Nothing can be accomplished with *such a body...* My body is too long for a its weakness, it hasn't the least bit of fat to engender a blessed warmth, to preserve an inner fire, no fat on which the spirit could occasionally nourish itself beyond its daily need without *damage to the whole*. How shall the *weak heart* that lately has troubled me so often be able to pound the blood through the length of these *legs*. It would be labor enough to the *knees*, and from there it can only spill with a senile strength into the lower parts of his legs. But now it is already needed up above again, it is being waited for, while it is wasting itself below. Everything is pulled apart throughout the length of my body. What could it accomplish then, when it perhaps wouldn't have enough strength for what I want to achieve even if it were shorter and more compact.[7]

The body in disease entails 'damage to the whole', a breakdown not only with the world around but also with one's own body. The wholeness of existence gives way to fragmentation and alienation; and this fragmentation and alienation is not only experienced psychologically but also corporeally. All of a sudden the body parts that we were oblivious to so far resurface and call for attention in the form of 'weak heart', 'knees' and 'legs'. The body and its parts in illness seem uncanny and foreign, distinguished from the wholeness of the self (being-with-the-world and being-with-the-body) that health *creates*.

---

[6] Franz Kafka, *Letters to Milena*, trans. Philip Boehm, (New York, Schocken, 1990), 169.
[7] Franz Kafka, *The Diaries*, ed. Max Brod, trans. Martin Greenberg and Hannah Arendt, (New York, Schocken, 1949), 160.

Kafka feels that his organs are conspiring against him and his (w)holistic existence. This conspiracy of the body parts which went on without his knowledge highlights the unhome-like existence of the body in illness and, this inability of keeping the "whole intact" is one of the chief characteristics of illness. Kafka writes:

> You see, my brain was unable to bear the pain and anxiety with which it had been burdened. It said: "I'm giving up; but if anyone else here cares about keeping the *whole intact*, then he should share the load and things will run a little longer." Whereupon my lung volunteered, it probably didn't have much to lose anyway. These negotiations between brain and lung, which went on without my knowledge, may well have been quite terrifying.[8]

He considers this *wholeness* as a form of deception because in health one is never aware of the daily drama of the body. The awareness comes with illness only. Health is a state of complete harmony so much so that it hinges on the level of ignorance when one is pre-reflectively involved with the world. It is often conceived as enigmatic and illusive in nature. The breakdown at the time of illness can in a way become an opportunity of reflection and awareness. It can pull us out of ignorance by bracketing our natural attitude(s) out. For Kafka, ignorance was never bliss:

> This state of health is also deceptive, it deceives even me; at any moment I am liable to be assailed by the most detailed and precise imaginings and invariably on the most inconvenient occasions.[9]

The fear of existence of uncanny body parts and the kind of relationship amongst them create a picture of Kafkaesque body which is no different from the Kafkaesque reality— a world of shame, guilt, fear and abhorrence. Kafka's attitude towards the diseased body is that of fear and abhorrence also. He himself detests sitting beside someone suffering from larynx. He writes to Max Brod on 11 March 1921:

> I am firmly convinced, now that I have been living here among consumptives, that healthy people run no danger of infection. Here, howev-

---

[8] Kafka, *Letters to Milena*, 162.
[9] Kafka, *Letters to Felice*, 425.

er, the healthy are only the wood cutters in the forest and the girls in the kitchen (who will simply pick uneaten food from the plates of patients and eat it—patients whom I *shrink* from sitting opposite) but not a single person from our town circles. But how *loathsome* it is to sit opposite a larynx patient, for instance (blood brother of a consumptive but far sadder), who sits across from you so friendly and harmless, looking at you with the transfigured eyes of the consumptive and at the same time coughing into your face through his spread fingers drops of purulent phlegm from his tubercular ulcer. At home I would be sitting that way, though not quite in so *dire* a state, as 'good uncle' among the children.[10]

His experience of living in a sanatorium amongst tubercular patients, as Kafka himself points out, is both *dire* and *loathsome*. He fails to establish any meaningful relationship with the inhabitants— his being cut-off from the other and from the world equidistantly. The dis-ease maintains the distance between the suffering being and the world, leading into a form of not only ghettoization but also of self-ghettoization; this means that in disease alienation is not always externally imposed: the sufferer alienates himself from the world also creating a ghetto of his own. The diseased body 'shrinks' as much as the diseased body 'shrinks itself'. The 'ecstatic' involvement in health, existing 'out of' its corporeality *shrinks* not only when one is ill but also when one suddenly encounters the 'other' in the form of any diseased and abjected body. It is simply based on such ideas that discourses, especially medical discourses were generated to reproduce the Jewish body along with the bodies of the gypsies and homosexuals as abnormal, diseased and deviant— the abjected 'other'.

Kafka's "anxiety of becoming what one is condemned to become"[11] is quite evident when he writes, "Without going into all the medical details, the outcome is that I have tuberculosis in both lungs. That I should suddenly develop some disease did not surprise me…"[12] and goes onto locating the corporeal disease in his prevalent psychological state. He continues, "…for years my insomnia and headaches have invited a serious illness"[13]. Tuberculosis, the disease he was suffering from, was as much physical as psychological, as he points in one of his letters, "I am mentally handicapped, the lung disease is none other than an overflow of the mental disease"[14]. Kafka here, though

---

[10] Kafka, *Letters to Friends, Family, and Editors*, 264.
[11] Sander Gilman, *Franz Kafka, the Jewish Patient*, (London, Routledge, 1995), 8.
[12] Kafka, *Letters to Milena*.
[13] Ibid.
[14] Ibid.

unwittingly, emphasizes the psychosomatic aspect of illness, any disease whether mental or corporeal is not exclusive either to the mind or the body. Susan Sontag points out the contemporary discourse built upon the analogies between tuberculosis and mental insanity: both TB and mental insanity results into confinement where the sufferers on diagnosis are sent to the institution called 'sanatorium'. The latter Sontag points out, entails a "common word for a clinic for tuberculars and the most common euphemism for an insane asylum"[15]. The sanatorium in both cases is a world in itself with its own governing rules and regulations. Both the diseases is an exile of some sort where Sontag highlights:

> The metaphor of the psychic voyage is an extension of the romantic idea of travel that was associated with tuberculosis. [...] It is not an accident that the most common metaphor for an extreme psychological experience viewed positively—whether produced by drugs or by becoming psychotic—is a trip.[16]

Locating mental illness on body and corporeal illnesses in mind are common practices even till today. The 'condemned' body of a Jew, therefore, was never far from his mental disposition and vice-versa. This *fin-de-siecle* medicalization and territorialization of the Jewish body, even years after Robert Koch's discovery, add complexities to the entire discourse paving the way for the construction and dissemination of the Jewish 'imagined' body. The 'condemned' body of the Jew was thus seen from a reductionist point of view, a bare body, pathological body to be dissected and incarcerated 'like a patient etherized on a table'.

But life is never bare, as Maurice Blanchot points out; what remains is "the naked relation to naked life"[17]. A man can be destroyed but what remains indestructible is his relation with alterity— the naked relation with the Other. Similarly, a body can never be bare completely for a long time. A subject— diseased, crippled and bare— almost at the threshold of collapse witnesses a flight of its subjectivity towards inter-subjectivity: an ethical, phenomenological and psychological 'escape' from enrootedness to a more collective relationality. This "extreme exposure and sensitivity of one's subjectivity to an-

---

[15] Sontag, *Illness as Metaphor*, 35-6.
[16] Ibid.
[17] Maurice Blanchot, *The Infinite Conversation*, trans. S. Hanson, (Minneapolis, University of Minnesota Press, 1993), 133.

other"[18] transcends the limits of human existence and vulnerability of a body-subject towards a more ethical inter-Being. The vulnerable body ceases to limit itself in its *Dasein* and becomes the site of Transcendence. What trigger this Transcendence are illness, shame and pain. Such kind of negation (*nichtung*) of the subjectivity is also a mode of self-consciousness.

Existence 'otherwise than being' is despite oneself in the midst of vulnerability. In pain, life is 'despite life'. This 'risky unconvering' of the self is painful and yet very sensible. It is this sensibility amidst vulnerability "that is an opening to others, a nearness, the one-for-the-other, precisely vulnerability to others"[19]. This pain which calls into question our very existence is what cuts through our finite skin exposing us to the scorching sun of the Infinite. Such inescapable relationship, *a relation without a relation*, with the infinite is what sustains life despite oneself: *life is life despite life.*

In illness, one is reduced to its corporeal existence which is nothing more than a lump of flesh. But this existential reduction also provides a way by which we can reflect both on our body and also the world around us. In health we tend to forget that our bodies are like anchors— anchoring us to the world; illness, on the other hand, makes us aware of our anchorages, spatio-temporal existence, our being being-in-the-world. The latter brings us to the simple fact that we *exist*. Illness enables us to reflect and take notice of the things which were hitherto absent. Actually painful and non-volitional, it can still provide a new meaning to our existence. Kafka shares the same opinion and writes:

> All these alleged diseases, sad as they may seem, are matters of faith, anchorages in some maternal ground for souls in distress.... those anchorages which are firmly fixed in real ground aren't merely isolated, interchangeable possessions—they are preformed in man's being, and they continue to form and re-form his being (as well as his body) along the same lines.[20]

He realizes that illnesses and diseases are integral parts of one's existence. They are not antithetical to life rather they are 'preformed in man's being, and they continue to form and re-form his being'. Illness then, becomes essential to not only one's being but also one's *becoming.*

---

[18] Levinas, *Existence and Existents*, (The Hague, Nijhoff, 1978).
[19] L. Benaroyo, "The notion of vulnerability in the philosophy of Emmanuel Levinas and its significance for medical ethics and aesthetics", (5 October 2014), http://www.api.or.at/aebm/download/docs/web_levinas.pdf2007
[20] Kafka, *Letters to Milena*, 216-217.

Kafka and his bleeding body: the body with all its flesh and blood and its embodiedness anticipates the condition of the Jewish body during the time of *Shoah*. The racialization and over-medicalization turned the Jewish body into a grotesque body— a body "that defies clear definitions and borders and that occupies the middle ground between life and death, between subject and object, between one and many"[21]; this kind of fluidity that Kafka "deciphers it with his wound"[22] and can be traced all over his oeuvre. The 'unfinished' and 'ambiguous' body of Kafka, suffering from bodily feebleness, somatic otherness, neurasthenia and tuberculosis, signify, as Sander Gilman points out, his existence as a Jewish body. Not only tuberculosis but the very pain and *angst* of living within the confinements of or rather beyond the boundaries of the societal arrangement lead to the creation of an alien and uncanny self-body. His was not a body that can be what Sartre[23] calls 'passed-over-in-silence', an inexperiential 'unaware awareness' but fleshly and corporeal, a body that can be put on trial, stigmatized and objectified and finally, destroyed. But it was also the same body with all its fleshliness and corporeality that enabled him and those like him into a non-closed, open and inter-corporeal subjectivity connected to others in the form of an ethical relationship— the "ever unfinished, ever creating body"[24].

"This excessive body which constantly outgrows itself and escapes from its own skin, constitutes a body that cannot be framed"[25]. It, though ambiguous and open, never dissolves into an inauthentic and undifferentiated oblivion but maintains its singularity and differentiation at all risk. The ethics and poetics, "overlapping and limit" of such bodies are always functional at the same time[26]. This is how the "grotesque", hyper- or de-politicized Jewish bodies and its "shared flesh", calls for a crisis in civilization by being 'unrepresentable' or 'unknowable'. "It comprises *singularity, heterogeneity* and *difference*"[27].

The will to power over the other, to limit its embodied intersubjectivity, lead to an ethical closure transforming the other into an Other— an opaque body which can be fixed but never assimilated. These 'unassimilated' bodies—

---

[21] Shabot, "Grotesque Bodies", 229.
[22] Kafka, *The Penal Colony*, 204.
[23] See Jean Paul Sartre, *Being and Nothingness An Essay on Phenomenological Ontology*, trans. Hazel E. Barnes, (New York, Broadway Books, 1958).
[24] Mikhail Bakhtin, *Rabelais and his World*, (Cambridge, MIT Press, 1965), 26.
[25] Shabot, "Groteque Bodies", 229.
[26] Maurice Merleau-Ponty, *The Visible and the Invisible*, (Evanston, Northwestern University Press, 1968), 142.
[27] Shabot, "Groteque Bodies", 231.

excesses of body and bodies of excess, can either be feared or despised, either be worshiped or exterminated depending upon the need of the hour. In those situations cruelties are justified; and radical medicalization is just another process of justification for maintaining social equilibrium (read, health). Those bodies, unclean and 'unfinished', become the site of politics of *excess* and *equilibrium* so much so that it becomes, what Luc-Nancy calls, "the desire for murder, for an increase of cruelty and horror... it is mutilation, carving up, relentlessness, meticulous execution, the joy of agony"[28]. The politics of excess and equilibrium, thus, give rise to the 'normal' and the 'pathological'.

The birth of pathology entailed the death of the body and what remained was a body entangled in the politics of sign and signification, an objectified body subject to examination and/or extermination. But Nancy has argued that "there has never been any body in philosophy"[29] and, what you have in place is a series of metaphors trying earnestly to get hold of the body and undoubtedly, the body in pain; the guilt from which not only the western metaphysics but also our language is suffering. He explains, "from the body-cave to the glorious body, signs have become inverted, just as they have been turned around and displaced over and over again, in hylomorphism, in the sinner-body, in the body-machine or in the 'body proper' of phenomenology. But the philosophical-theological corpus of bodies is still supported by the spine of mimesis, of representation, and of the sign"[30]. The Jewish body— the body in 'pain' (derived from the Greek word *poin* and Latin word *poena* both meaning punishment, torture and penalty), in a similar vein remained the unknown and unrepresentable body down the ages till efforts were launched in the twentieth-century to expose it completely and examine it to be the pathological, parasitic and punishable body. Kafka in a letter to Max Brod writes: "And there is a relationship between all this and Jewishness, or more precisely between young Jews and their Jewishness, with the fearful inner predicament of these generations."[31]

The *presence* of the Jewish body "embedded in the material world characterized by its spatial, tangible relations"[32]— its lived (embodied) experience of history and politics, the 'being in touch', helped its movement away from

---

[28] Jean Luc-Nancy, *Being Singular Plural*, trans. Robert D. Richardson and Anne E. O'Bryne, (Stanford, Stanford University Press), 21.
[29] Luc-Nancy, *Corpus*, 193.
[30] Ibid, 192.
[31] Kafka, *Letters to Friends, Family and Editors*.
[32] Hans Ulrich Gumbrecht, *Production of Presence: What Meaning Cannot Convey*, (Stanford, Stanford University Press, 2004), 318.

complete biological reductionism or constructivism and medicalization or racialization of being (*ousia*). The discipline of medicine, as Long suggests, seeks to objectify the body while the discipline of historiography objectifies the past— and as a consequence what results into is the circumcised history of the circumcised body[33]. In this 'somatic turn', Kafka then emerges as a brilliant study of the history of the flesh and the history in the flesh, a perfect paradigm of how crises of representation led to a crisis in civilization in the twentieth century.

Works Cited

Bakhtin, M. *Rabelais and His World*. Cambridge: The MIT Press. 1965.

Benaroyo, L. "The notion of vulnerability in the philosophy of Emmanuel Levinas and its significance for medical ethics and aesthetics", (5 October 2014), http://www.api.or.at/aebm/download/docs/web_levinas.pdf2007

Blanchot, M. *The Infinite Conversation*. Trans. S. Hanson. Minneapolis: University of Minnesota Press. 1993.

Corbin, A. *The Foul and the Fragrant: Odor and the French Social Imagination*. Cambridge: Harvard UP. 1986.

Deleuze, G., Guattari, F. *Kafka: Toward a Minor Literature*. Minneapolis: University of Minnesota Press. 1986.

Gilman, Sander L. *Franz Kafka, the Jewish Patient*. London: Routledge. 1995.

Gilman, Sander L. *Franz Kafka: Critical Lives*. London: Reaktion Books. 2005.

Kafka, Franz. *Letters to Friends, Family, and Editors*.Ed. Max Brod.Trans. Richard and Clara Winston. New York: Schocken. 1977.

Kafka, Franz. *Letters to Felice*.Ed. Erich Heller and Jurgen Born.Trans. James Stern and Elizabeth Duckworth. New York: Schocken. 1973.

Kafka, Franz. *Letters to Milena*.Trans. Philip Boehm. New Yok: Schocken. 1990.

Kafka, Franz. *Letters to Ottla and the Family*. Ed. N. N. Glatzer. Trans. Richard and Clara Winston. New York: Schocken. 1982.

Levinas, Emmanuel. *Otherwise than Being or Beyond Essence*.Trans. AlphonsoLingis.The Netherlands: Kluwer Academic Press. 1981.

Levinas, Emmanuel. *Existence and Existents*. The Hague: Nijhoff. 1978.

Long, L. *Rehabilitating Bodies: Health, History, and the American Civil War*. Philadelphia: University of Pennsylvania. 2004.

Merleau-Ponty, Maurice. *The Visible and the Invisible*. Evanston: Northwestern University Press. 1968.

Nancy, Jean Luc. *Being Singular Plural*. Trans. Robert D. Richardson and Anne E. O'Byrne. Stanford, California: Stanford University Press. 2000.

---

[33] For more discussion on the subject, refer L. Long, *Rehabilitating Bodies: Health, History, and the American Civil War*, (Philadelphia, University of Pennsylvania, 2004).

Nancy, Jean-Luc. *Corpus*. trans. Richard Rand. New York: Fordham University Press. 2008.

Sartre, Jean Paul. *Being and Nothingness: An Essay on Phenomenological Ontology*. Trans. Hazel E. Barnes. London: Routledge.1958.

Shabot, Sara Cohen. "Grotesque Bodies: A Response to Disembodied Cyborgs". *Journal of Gender Studies*.Vol.15, 2006. pp. 223-235.

Sontag, Susan. *Illness as Metaphor.*New York: Vintage Books. 1978.

Chapter 3

'Connoisseurship... of Disease' and Thomas Mann's *Death in Venice*

What were art and virtue to him given the advantages of *chaos*?

-Mann

Gustav von Aschenbach's struggle to remain an artist and his search for new artistic avenues overlap with his biological decay, dying and subsequent death in Venice. The narrative captures his dilemma between the Apollonian and Dionysian impulses, his repressed homoerotic desires, his suffering from writer's block and cholera, and treating them single-handedly and locating them on a singular yet variedly symptomatic body. Thomas Mann's interest in disease which, sometimes, was often at the brink of obsession hindered him from portraying illness and disease in his works as mere metaphorical usage. Hence, we should not read cholera's victimisation of Aschenbach in this novella as merely an allegory of the protagonist's spiritual decay. The metaphysical understanding of disease will rather be kept at bay in our analysis of Mann's *Death in Venice* (1912). While discussing about the harrowing effects of cholera on human body William H. McNeill in his *Plagues and Peoples* points out the rate with which cholera spread and how it is difficult not to panic in the face of this sudden death. And apart from this, "the symptoms" he highlights "were particularly horrible: radical dehydration meant that a victim shrank into a wizened caricature of his former self within a few hours, while ruptured capillaries discoloured the skin, turning it black and blue"[1]— where one harrowing event leads to another harrowing result in which,

> to make mortality uniquely visible: patterns of bodily decay were exacerbated and accelerated, as in a time-lapse motion picture, to remind all who saw it of death's ugly horror and utter inevitability.[2]

---

[1] William H. McNeill, *Plagues and Peoples*, (New York, Quality Paperback, 1993), 261.
[2] Ibid.

In Mann's *Death in Venice*, Aschenbach's body juxtaposes biological decay, repressed desire, and *dépaysement*— the state of being in a foreign, unfamiliar land. Our bodies are as much ours' as they belong to others. They are *ekstatically* with the world. Unlike other objects our bodies are never elemental and singular; they are plural and are continuously influenced by multiple external factors. The body is as much into the environment as the environment is into the body and yet, it is not an airy nothing. It never loses its essential characteristics. As we travel the body undergoes changes also and gets influenced by various factors— geographical, clinical, gastronomical, cultural et cetera— and yet does not undergo a complete transformation. In its efforts at becoming-other, it never forgets its being. Aschenbach's travel to Venice and his efforts of becoming Venetian will never be complete as he will never be able to erase the imprints of the past. He will never be able to *reach* Venice. He will always be a traveler (the word travel derives from the French 'travail' meaning work) working *on* the body as much as *with* the body[3].

This sense of (non)ending is what haunts our protagonist from the very beginning but, at the same time, enables him to understand his *true* self. Also, Aschenbach's sense of non-ending, his knowledge of *unreachability*, meets his sense of ending and *ability* later in the work. It was his awareness of death as a way to be and not as a way to end that brings him closer to truth and what it means to *be*. Death, here, reveals itself not as negative or as antithetical to life but as something that entails meaningful possibilities. It was his awareness of death that finally helps him to overcome his fear of (non)ending and exist *authentically*.

Mann's treatment of Tadzio, Venice and death are on the same plane. We see the metaphor of death used over and over again in the context of describing Tadzio and Venice. The necropolis of Venice has been represented no differently from the morbid Tadzio. Aschenbach while reflecting on Tadzio says, "He is delicate, he is sickly" and again, "He will most likely not live to grow old" (27). Initially, Tadzio, Venice and death were all covered with the cloak of mystery and Aschenbach was alienated from all of them equidistantly. But it was his realization of mortality and death that finally revealed the actuality before him. The endeavour of knowing one's self finally culminated into one's death. For Aschenbach, the moment of ultimate truth conflates with his moment of death. This transformation from concealment to revelation, from someone who feared death to a 'being-towards-death' is what constitutes *Death in Venice*. Instead of considering death as an end or an incident that

---

[3] Jonathan Gill Harris, *The First Firangis*, (India, Aleph Books, 2015), 10.

happens in future, Mann sees death as an existential awareness of the possible not-being. Death here becomes a phenomenon of life that reveals the way in which a human being exists and what it means to be. It was his alienation from death during the course of the narrative that made Aschenbach *foreign* to Tadzio, to Venice and, most importantly, to himself.

Living and dying are two sides of the same coin. They are not antithetical to each other depending upon how we see; concealing one would be equivalent to alienating a part of your 'self'. In his effort to conceal his physical signs of ageing and look young Aschenbach started visiting a salon. Going to the barber was his attempt to highlight only the *living* side of his existence while concealing the *dying* side. But as long as he did that he always remained something not-yet. He failed to realize the *end* as an indelible part of one's own being and led a self-alienating life— it was Aschenbach's death in Venice that finally revealed to him the other side, the side from which he was alienated for the most part of his life. His attempt to look young was a mere façade. Mann in his essay 'Goethe and Tolstoy' writes, that "[t]he human form can never be grasped merely through the observation of its surface; one must uncover its inner being, separate its parts, note the connections between them"[4]. His *Death in Venice*, thus, is a journey that a writer undertakes towards the unknown— the ultimate— and the infinite resulting in his *Erziehung*: writing is but life in disguise and life is but death in disguise. The narrative juxtaposes art, life, dying and death in a way that they all become a part of a 'zone of indistinction'.

Aschenbach's love and death wish for Tadzio and his love and death wish for himself establish a very uncanny relation which he shares with both life and death. His expressions of love and life were never free from thanatological signifiers. Moreover, instead of fleeing from the site he embraces plague as the last resort to be with the boy. The narrator points out,

> Aschenbach sometimes thought that through departure or death everyone else could be removed so that he could remain alone with the beautiful on the island... (49)

The fear of oblivion mingled with the wish for oblivion makes the entire trajectory an ambiguous one. This tête-a-tête with the other is both loathed and desired at the same time and it is a disease that enables this encounter. In the novella, cholera becomes the borderline between Aschenbach's self and not-

---

[4] See Clayton Koelb, *Thomas Mann's "Goethe and Tolstoy": Notes and Sources*, (Alabama, University of Alabama Press, 1984), 205.

self. It brings him close to the other— understanding of which is pivotal to the understanding one's own existence. "Surrendering", as Arthur W. Frank notes while referring to Audrey Lorde's *The Cancer Journal*, "the superficial control of health yields control of a higher order. Lorde expresses this paradox when she writes that only by facing death can she become someone over whom no one has power."[5] The same can be said about that of Gustav von Aschenbach.

Mann's emphasis on the Dionysian impulses of the disordered body and its effect on the psychosomatic condition of Aschenbach are conveyed through cholera:

> There he sat, the master; this was he who had found a way to reconcile art and honours; who had written The Abject, in a style of classic purity renounced bohemianism and all its works, all sympathy with the abyss and the troubled depths of the outcast human soul. This was he who had put knowledge underfoot to climb so high; who had outgrown the ironic pose and adjusted himself to the burdens and obligations of fame; whose renown had been officially recognized and his name ennobled, whose style was set for a model in the schools. There he sat. His eyelids were closed, there was only a swift, sidelong glint of the eyeballs now and again, something between a question and a leer; while the rouged and flabby mouth uttered single words of the sentences shaped in his disordered brain by the fantastic logic that governs our dreams. (51)

It is through the plagued body of Aschenbach that Mann raises some fundamental issues pertinent to both human existence and aesthetics. He notes that *"disease makes men more physical, it leaves them nothing but body"*[6].He writes further that *"And now his body has come into the foreground in another sense and made itself important and independent of the rest of him, namely— through illness"*[7]. The significance that he attributes to the diseased body is grounded in Schopenhauer's paradoxical appreciation of the body as a seat of 'pain and deficiency' and as 'the ground of our knowledge'. The disordered and diseased body then becomes a mechanism to know the self. Schopen-

---

[5] Arthur W. Frank, *The Wounded Storyteller: Body, Illness, Ethics*, (Chicago, The University Press of Chicago, 1995), 126.
[6] Thomas Mann, *The Magic Mountain*, trans. H. T. Lowe Porter, (London, Vintage, 1999), 178.
[7] Ibid, 184.

hauer was cynical of the perception of disease as an 'accidental error' within the 'manageable machine' that the body has become.

Aschenbach as a foreigner (one who is 'not familiar'), and his *foreignness* becomes the very symptom of the kind of alienation that he was suffering from. His journey from homelike status quo to a strange un-homelike foreign space is a metaphor of the kind of transition his body was going through— from the state of healthy being-in-the-world to the state of illness. Though this was not his first visit to Venice, his unfamiliarity of the place can be seen as a de-worldling and, as Rebecca Saunders points out, "requires a thematization that is not necessary for the native, orientation must be learned and considered, belongingness takes deliberation"[8]. His phenomenological un-familiarity with Venice is evident from the fact that it was always an exotic, distant and uncanny place to him. He could never involve himself with the place and the people. Now, the kind of *de-worldling* from which he was afflicted involves two things: Saunders points out that, "first, it likens foreigners to entities not characterized by *Dasein*, associates them with non-being, animals, instrumental objects, and material goods. Second, it evinces the degree to which foreignness is commensurate with physical pain; for Elaine Scarry has argued, 'the absence of pain is a presence of world; the presence of pain is the absence of world'."[9] The body which is supposed to act as a bridge between the self and the world, in case of Aschenbach was acting as a hindrance. He was finding it difficult to get involved with the world *bodily* (which is an important criterion for *Dasein*). He was completely out of place. His entire world was infested and subsumed by cholera. Lisa Sanders in her *Every Patient Tells a Story* makes an important point in this regard, "[t]he experience of being ill can be like waking up in a foreign country. Life, as you formerly knew it, is on hold while you travel through this other world as unknown as it is unexpected."[10]

The process of *de-worldling* also, paradoxically, enabled Aschenbach to understand reality in greater degree as he started reflecting on things more clearly and objectively. This 'breakdown' enabled a dialogue, eradicating 'the automatism of perception' and helping him to overcome the kind of estrangement and alienation that he was suffering from. The kind of *anxiety* that this uncanny situation led can be grasped with the help of the German

---

[8] Rebecca Saunders, "Keeping a Distance: Heidegger and Derrida on foreignness and friends", *Angelaki Vol.16*, no.2, (June 2011): 37.
[9] Ibid.
[10] Lisa Sanders, *Every Patient Tells a Story: Medical Mysteries and the Art of Diagnosis*, (New York, Broadway Books, 2009).

word *ungeheur*[11]. "It is" as Hans-Georg Gadamer points out, "people's disposition of anxiety that the question of the meaning of being and the meaning of nothingness visible in a new way"[12]. He was no more oblivious and unaware; he was no more 'pre-reflectively' involved with the world. Instead of being only the reason for his suffering and death cholera was also instrumental in his emancipation for it absorbed and intensified life meanings and facilitated a better understanding of both life and death. It worked as an *anagnorisis*. Susan Sontag in her *Illness as Metaphor* points out that "Cholera is the kind of fatality that, in retrospect, has simplified a complex self"[13]. As long as he was alive, he was always something 'not-yet'. The existential mood of anxiety that death brought helped him to appreciate life holistically. His life was complete by death. It brought the possibility to impossibility, it brought infinitive to his finite existence.

Instead of considering *Death in Venice* as "Mann's attempt to recapturing the classical explanation for disease, which allows Aschenbach to be absolved of his sins through disease", cholera in this novella should be considered as a mode of emancipation towards knowledge. Nicola Von Bodman-Hensler points out that "[w]ithin Mann's thinking falling ill thus means in a first instance the immersion in nature, whilst also granting the possibility of emancipation from nature through this experience of immersion. This stance hints at the valourisation of defect as the sign of a successful process of immersion"[14]. The way the diseased body has been seen in the novella marks the transition from medical to aesthetic gaze. The aesthetic transformation— from Apollonian to Dionysian— through which Aschenbach undergoes, then, becomes a metaphor for the paradigmatic shift from science to art and, the way the former and the latter look at the body and its disorderliness.

Illness is the night side of Aschenbach's life. It brought the much-needed *chaos* to his apparently structured and ordered social life. Mann himself says: "what were art and virtue to him given the advantages of *chaos*?"[15] Health is,

---

[11] Gadamer defines *ungeheur* as "a highly effective expression for the incomprehensible vastness, for the emptiness, remoteness and strangeness which takes our breath away even while we struggle to sustain our lives and to make ourselves at home in this world." Hans-Georg, *The Enigma of Health*, (California, Stanford University Press, 1996), 154.
[12] Ibid, 153.
[13] Sontag, *Illness as Metaphor*, 37.
[14] Nicola Von Bodman-Hensler, "Thomas Mann's Illness Mythologies in the Work of Philip Roth" (PhD diss., King's College London, 2013), 26.
[15] Thomas Mann, *Thomas Mann's 'Goethe and Tolstoy': Notes and Sources*, (Alabama, University of Alabama Press, 1984), 205.

on the other hand often associated with wholeness and harmony. The Dionysian illness to which he succumbs and the Apollonian aesthetics in which he believed makes Aschenbach's heart cleave in twain. Ritchie Robertson points out how in Chapter 2 the two dimensions of Aschenbach become quite visible: the classical and the Romantic. The classicism, for poets like Goethe and Schiller, Robertson points out meant "the physical health and harmony, the sense of being happily at home in the world, that they ascribed to the Greeks. Aschenbach is far removed from such an ideal. His health is poor. His substantial oeuvre is the product of determined self-discipline which enabled him to use all his available strength for literary work". He elaborates further how also Aschenbach's,

> frail physical powers, including his creative energies, are controlled by an iron will. His feminine, intuitive abilities, his maternal inheritance, are under the firm guidance of his masculine, rational character: at least until the experience of homosexual love dissolves the rigid antitheses which frame his life.[16]

Philosophically, order and disorder, cosmos and chaos, *archē* and *anarchē* are not indifferent from each other. The classical limitation and the romantic transgression made Aschenbach a dual citizen of the life-world. Hence, Aschenbach's romantic yearning for the Mediterranean is a result of his illness. The Northerners finally succumbing to the sexual impulses in the South is a very common phenomenon in literature, of which E.M. Forster and Oscar Wilde, as Robertson points out, are best examples.[17]

Mann's philosophy is not that of *melete thanatou* (a 'practice of death'). He does not consider the 'soul' to be a prisoner of the body; for him, the body is not a site of pain, desire, anguish, suffering and estrangement. Unlike Plato, he does not believe that "the supreme gnosis of being is only possible in a state of complete freedom from the body and its distractions and constraints"[18]. Rather, his notion of freedom is always already embodied. He is not of the view that one should detach "his or her psyche from what Bergson called 'the plane of life'". Aschenbach's moment of death for Mann thus is not

---

[16] Ritchie Robertson, "Classicism and its Pitfalls: *Death in Venice*", *The Cambridge Companion to Thomas Mann*, (Cambridge, Cambridge University Press, 2004), 98.
[17] Ibid, 96.
[18] Michael Grosso, "Plato's Phaedo and the Near-Death Experience: Survival Research and Self-Transformation" in *Death and Dying*, ed. Sudhir Kakar (India, Penguin Books, 2014), 53.

the moment when the mind/soul severs all ties from the body but, a moment of truth and consummation— a moment when life becomes complete. Aschenbach, while dying had a renewed sense of perception and wonder of the world, a feeling heightened by the prospect of an ending. Mann's idea of body, illness and death was thus more romantic. Like Keats' "at the foundation" of Mann's work "is the paradox that life accrues value precisely to the extent that one intensely experiences its fragility and transience. Or, as the twentieth-century American poet Wallace Stevens put it in his most Keatsian poem: 'Death is the mother of beauty'."[19] The following statement by Mann is more romantic than anything: "Symptoms of disease are nothing but a disguised manifestation of the power of love; and all disease is only love transformed" (*The Magic Mountain*). And again: "Solitude gives birth to the original in us, to beauty unfamiliar and perilous - to poetry. But also, it gives birth to the opposite: to the perverse, the illicit, the absurd" (*Death in Venice*). Like Romantics, he regards death as both an end and a mode of emancipation. In him, we see both denial and acceptance of death. The "perverse, the illicit, the absurd" here is the Dionysian to which our protagonist finally succumbs.

Aschenbach transforms his denial of death into a denial of rage against death. He refuses to rage against 'the dying of the light' and finally, accepts death with peace and equanimity:

> He rested his head against the chair-back and followed the movements of the figure out there, then lifted it, as it were in answer to Tadzio's gaze. It sank on his breast, the eyes looked out beneath their lids, while his whole face took on the relaxed and brooding expression of deep slumber. It seemed to him the pale and lovely Summoner out there smiled at him and beckoned; as though, with the hand he lifted from his hip, he pointed outward as he hovered on before into an immensity of richest expectation. And, as so often before, he rose to follow.
>
> Some minutes passed before anyone hastened to the aid of the elderly man sitting there collapsed in his chair.... (52)

Tadzio and Venice were mere catalysts in this transformation. They first heightened and, finally, resolved all the conflicts. "One does this by" as Michael Grosso points out "pursuing a path of dialectic that leads from dianoia

---

[19] Ronald A. Sharp, "Sorrow More Beautiful than Beauty's Self': John Keats and the Music of Self" in *Death and Dying*, ed. Sudhir Kakar (India, Penguin Books, 2014), 73.

(conceptual understanding) to direct mystical illumination or nous"[20]. He now really thinks it is a *good* night. Marie de Hennezel, a French psychologist, believes and her belief can be related to Aschenbach and that is: "the person who says to someone else 'I am going to die' does not become the *victim* of death but, rather, the *protagonist* in his or her own dying"[21].

His quest for peace brings him to Venice. But contrary to his expectation Venice catapults Aschenbach more towards his hidden and tabooed desires— his not yet acknowledged self. He is suddenly dragged out of his comfort zone (read, the pre-reflective lived-space) and made to encounter his own other, the part which was hitherto latent. Aschenbach's mourning at the end should be seen as a way of laying things to rest. His acceptance of death is nothing more than a way of mourning the loss of whatever he used to cherish— his health, his writings, his Apollonian stature et al. The pathological condition of melancholia here is remitted by the recognition of his relation with death and dying. The sense of mortality, sharpened by the radical nature of illness, provides him with new perspectives and dislodging the natural attitude and habit. In such circumstances, one does not try to evade death as a futural event but regard it as a mode of existential attitude and a source of anxiety essential for one's becoming, of one's fullest realization. Taking a cue from Kierkegaard, Gosetti-Ferencei notes in her article 'Death and Authenticity', "Anxiety, in a call from nowhere that seems to be inescapable, catches up with *Dasein*, and shakes up *Dasein* with a call of conscience such that facing death, or facing mortality and the most extreme possibility, becomes possible"[22]. It was his anxiety of death and not fear that finally unbinds Aschenbach and makes him encounter his utmost potentialities. The possibility of death is one of the prerequisites of *potentiality-for-Being*[23]. She observes further that "In anxiety I do not know when or how I will die, but I do know only that I will die"[24]. Becoming estranges life and then appears in a novel way.

---

[20] Grosso, "Plato's 'Phaedo and Near-Death Experience", 44-69.
[21] For more details, see Marie de Hennezel, *Seize the Day: How the Dying teach us to live.* trans. Carol Brown Janeway, (London, Pan Macmillan, 2012).
[22] Jennifer Anna Gosetti-Ferencei, "Death and Authenticity: Reflections on Heidegger, Rilke, Blanchot", *Existenz Vol. 9/1*, (2014): 55.
[23] Heidegger writes in *Being and Time* "As potentiality-for-Being, Dasein cannot outstrip the possibility of death. Death is the possibility of the absolute impossibility of Dasein." from Martin Heidegger, *Being and Time*, trans. John Macquirre and Edward Robinson, (New York: Harper & Row, 1962), 294.
[24] Gosetti-Ferencei, "Death and Authenticity", 55.

Aschenbach's *ars moriendi* ('art of dying') is a critique of modernity's understanding of dying and death, and its project of prolonging dying instead of prolonging life. His death is unlike 'medical death'— "the technological prolongation of life at the expense of any real sense of the quality of life"[25]. His idea of 'where' to die and 'for whom' to die is quite apparent, unlike his 'how' to die; the poetics of 'how' to die in Aschenbach's case has its own logic very different from that of the conventional model. Anne Hunsaker Hawkins in her *Reconstructing Illness* refers to such pathographical and thanatographical accounts where the *Moriens* ('the dying person') device their own plot of dying and refuse to succumb to kafkaesque medical trials. In one such account, Eric Robinson writes that "Death is a personal experience and each one of us should be allowed to die his or her death and not to be expected to conform to some general pattern" [26]. The illness, dying and death of Aschenbach, thus, does not conform to the 'general pattern' of the modern health care system and re-evaluates the notion of "medical death". His illness and dying put forward of what I call 'the death of clinic'[27]—a process of de-medicalisation— a process to resist and subvert medical modernity and reclaim what, Henri Bergson in his *Creative Evolution* calls élan vital.

Works Cited

Bergson, Henri. *Creative Evolution*. USA: Sheba Blake Publishing, 2015.
Foucault, Michel. *The Birth of the Clinic*. London: Routledge, 1997.
Frank, Arthur W. *The Wounded Storyteller: Body, Illness, and Ethics*. Chicago: The University of Chicago Press, 1995.
Gadamer, Hans-Georg. *The Enigma of Health*. California: Stanford University Press, 1996.
Gosetti-Ferencei, Jennifer Anna. 'Death and Authenticity: Reflections on Heidegger, Rilke, Blanchot'. *ExistenzVol*. 9/1, 2014.53-62.
Harris, Jonathan Gill. *The First Firangis: Remarkable Stories of Heroes, Healers, Charlatans, Courtesans and other Foreigners who Became Indian*. India: Aleph Books. 2015.
Hawkins, Anne Hunsaker. *Reconstructing Illness: Studies in Illness*. Indiana: Purdue University Press, 1999.
Heidegger, Martin. *Being and Time*. Trans. John Macquarrie and Edward Robinson. New York: Harper & Row, 1962.

---

[25] Hawkins, *Reconstructing Illness*, 91.
[26] Ibid, 92.
[27] I am here referring to 'the death of the clinic' as opposed to Foucauldian 'the birth of the clinic'; the latter entails institutionalized and disciplined medical narrative.

Hennezel, Marie de. *Seize the Day: How the Dying teach us to live.* Trans. Carol Brown Janeway. London: Pan Macmillan, 2012.

Kakkar, Sudhir. Ed. *Death and Dying.* India: Penguin Books, 2012.

Mann, Thomas. *Death in Venice.* Trans. Stanley Appelbaum. New York: Dover Publications, Inc. 1995.

Mann, Thomas. *Thomas Mann's "Goethe and Tolstoy": Notes and Sources.* Ed. Clayton Koelb. Alabama: University of Alabama Press, 1984.

Mann, Thomas. *The Magic Mountain,* Trans. H. T. Lowe Porter. London: Vintage, 1999.

McNeill, William H. *Plagues and Peoples.* New York: Quality Paperbacks, 1993.

Nicola Von Bodman-Hensler, "Thomas Mann's Illness Mythologies in the Work of Philip Roth" (PhD diss., King's College London, 2013), 26.

Robertson, Ritchie. *The Cambridge Companion to Thomas Mann.* Cambridge: Cambridge University Press, 2004.

Sanders, Lisa. *Every Patient Tells a Story: Medical Mysteries and the Art of Diagnosis.* New York: Broadway Books, 2009.

Chapter 4

'Undiscovered Countries' with Virginia Woolf's *On Being Ill*

> [T]his monster, the body, this miracle, its pain, will soon make us taper into *mysticism*, or, rise with rapid beats of the wings, into the raptures of *transcendentalism*.
>
> -Virginia Woolf, On Being Ill

On Being Ill, the 1926 essay by Virginia Woolf trace her solitary journey into the unknown and distant country of illness where the destination and map with the help of which she used to navigate before were no longer relevant[1]. This sudden distantiation from the 'army of the upright', from the ideology of health, transcends her to a whole new paradigm of being-in-the-world. Illness in her case not only exerts a tyranny of pain and suffering but also a mode of reflection and seeing things in new light. Her life long battle with excruciating and debilitating psychosomatic illnesses is not something to which she succumbs but sublimates and sublates those agonizing affects into creative and liberating effects. She often associates it with mystical qualities: while staying in bed, she imagines herself seeing the whole of her work *The Waves*. She believes,

> these illnesses are in my case— how shall I express it?— partly mystical. Something happens in my mind. It refuses to go registering impressions. It shuts itself up. It becomes a chrysalis. I lie quite torpid, often with acute physical pain— as last year; only discomfort this. Then something *springs*.[2]

Illness, according to Woolf, is a journey of a solitary mind accompanied by none. It is not a shared experience and does not follow 'cooperative conventions'; firstly, because of the confinement it leads to and secondly, because of

---

[1] In illness, Judith Zaruch notes "the destination and map I had used to navigate before were no longer useful"; from Frank, *The Wounded Storyteller*, 1.
[2] Virginia Woolf, *A Writer's Diary: Being and Extracts from the Diary of Virginia Woolf*, ed. Leonard Woolf, (San Diego: A Harvest Book, 1954), 150.

the failure of language to capture the emotion associated with it— "Here we go alone, and like it better so", she writes (12). The healthy and normative continuum of being-with-the-world is challenged in illness exposing the very nudity of the self— a self which concomitantly becomes unipolar and concentrated. It is like "a whole current of life cut off". This alienated being cut-off from the world is an important aspect of illness. Moreover, the binary between *normal* and *abnormal*, the politics of segregation and social hygiene, were enforced quite violently in Europe in the first half of the twentieth century. Modern medicine, at the same time, by shifting its focus from the sufferer to the disease itself, alienates the person who is suffering throwing her into solitary incarceration. In modern medical discourse the *voice* of the sufferer remains unacknowledged and, quite often, the muteness of the sufferer mingles with the deafness of the healer. The alienating and dehumanizing gaze of modern medicine and the disjuncture that illness yields are represented metaphorically through this lonesome journey.

Illness diagnoses the very poverty of language when it comes to representing the pain and agony of suffering. Illness does not only resist formal language but destroys it completely, "deconstructing it into the pre-language of cries and groans"[3]. "English" Woolf points out, "which can express the thoughts of Hamlet and the tragedy of Lear, has no word for the shiver and the headache" (6). This gives an opportunity for her to call for a new breed of bodily language which will be more grotesque and carnivalised— "more primitive, more sensual, more obscene"— breaking the polite discourse of formal language (7). Herein language the politics of *equilibrium* gives way to the politics of *excess*. Such 'linguistic turn' will only be able to capture the daily drama of the body: of how love takes a backseat,

> [...] in favour of a temperature of 104; jealousy give place to the pangs of sciatia; sleeplessness play the part of villain, and the hero become the white liquid with a sweet taste— that mighty Prince with the moth's eye and the feathered feet, one of whose name is Chloral (7-8).

In this essay too the formal and classical structure has been challenged in favour of an almost plotless, wayward and impetuous narrative dealing with varied subjects and ideas. Such playfulness comes from the fact that her writing is more *through* the body and less *about* the body and more *through* illness and less *about* illness. Her writing then becomes very symptomatic of the grotesque body— the body in pain and suffering— materializing it into

---

[3] See Scarry, *Body in Pain*, 172.

text. The grotesque and complex "lump of pure sound" is crushed with pain to create "a brand new word" which quite often evokes laughter (7). The symptoms of illness are meanings in themselves and cannot be standardized.

By writing *through* the body she is trying to destabilize the dualism and the hierarchized structure prevalent in western metaphysics, of the body being a slave to the mind. She is, rather, pointing towards a grey zone of non-dualism when she says, "… [mind] cannot separate off from the body like a sheath of a knife or pod of a pea for a single instant"(4). A lived-body or a psychosomatic whole does not adhere to the Manichean binary which philosophy since pre-Socratic times has practiced. Philosophy always talks about "doings of the mind" and "how the mind has civilized the universe"(5). And body, on the other hand, has been kicked "like an old leather football, across leagues of snow and desert in the pursuit of conquest or discovery" (ibid). Woolf in this essay tries to materialize the mind and spiritualize the body. The mind and the body are too much into each other to be dealt with separately and differently. This (in)distinction is generally deemed as lived-body (*leib*) as opposed to a passive 'leather football' called corporeal body (*körpor*). And this dynamic lived-body "must go through the whole unending procession of changes, heat and cold, comfort and discomfort, hunger and satisfaction, health and illness, until there comes the inevitable catastrophe; the body smashes itself to smithereens, and the soul (it is said) escapes" (ibid). As long as we are alive, the body cannot be kicked off like an old leather football. The body should be ignored at its own peril. This essay and, in a way, her illness become an effort to go back to the body.

The 'daily drama of the body', according to Woolf, should not be overwhelmed by the 'doings of the mind'. Her writing successfully captures the more primitive sound of the body— the cries and groans— and gives it a voice. The absence of the body in western philosophy disturbs her a lot as she thinks our being-in-the-world as always already embodied. There is no disembodied consciousness. But the ideology of health throws the body into a state of oblivion. Taking the opportunity of a harmonious and holistic existence of the holy trinity of mind-body-world, the mind-self takes the body for granted "kicking the body…across leagues of snow and desert"(ibid). Across metaphysics, we see a reference to the body *in absentia*. This absent-body suddenly comes to the foreground when we are ill especially, in case of physical illness. In illness there occurs a dialogue where the body starts to speak to you (though in a very pre-linguistic, primordial manner) and the understanding of which requires dislodging our natural attitude in favour of a more radical reflection. Husserl would call this 'intentional feeling'. In order to avert the 'doings of the mind' we first have to do away with the natural and shared attitude (or rather a mere suspension of it). Illness helps in bracketing-out such attitudes.

Illness, as Havi Carel points out, not only entails rupture in the *contents* but *structure* of the experience too. It forces us to reflect on the things which were hitherto ignored. The daily drama of the body which was hitherto overwhelmed by the daily humdrum resurfaces to break down the whole structure of the everyday. In illness the continuum of time is replaced by individual moments and everyday is replaced by every day. One starts reflecting on the self and the world differently, as they appear now estranged and in a novel manner. In a painful and non-volitional way, illness creates this *difference*. In that sense, illness can also become a philosophical apparatus (this sounds uncanny, though). Carel explains how as opposed to the common philosophical methods which are volitional, illness is "uninvited and threatening"[4]. Illness, she explains:

> throws the ill person into a state of anxiety and uncertainty. As such it can be viewed as a radical, violent philosophical motivation that can profoundly alter our outlook. I argue that the radical nature of illness should be utilized to sharpen and expand philosophical discussion[5].

Like Husserlian *epoché*, it can challenge the prevalent pre-reflective and metaphysical discourses and can become an embodied 'philosophical gate' through which horizons of understanding and new philosophical encounters can be expanded and established.

The world seems *different* in illness. The corporeal enlightenment it leads to shuns the ignorance and alienation of a healthy being-in-the-world. The harmony of existence is challenged and replaced by the *disharmony* of phenomenological shock and revelation. Woolf does not beg to differ: "[n]ow, lying recumbent, staring straight up, the sky is discovered to be something so different from this that really it is a little *shocking*" (13). Here a Romantic existential expectation of empathy, harmony and integrated community gives way to a more radical outlook based on dis-integration or rather dys-integration. The Romantic empathy of sitting and hearing 'each other groan' is substituted by a Modernist disjuncture and 'disinterestedness'. Such dis-integration and dis-involvement are prerequisites for any phenomenological understanding leading to what Merleau-Ponty has called the "wonder in the face of the world"[6]; Woolf would call this "strange" and "shocking". One may

---

[4] Havi Carel, "The Philosophical Role of Illness", *Metaphilosophy Vol. 45*, (1995): 20-40
[5] Ibid.
[6] For more detailed discussions, see Maurice Merleau-Ponty, *Phenomenology of Perception*, trans. C. Smith, (New York, Routledge, 1962).

not feel-like-at-home and the world may seem strange and unfamiliar; Woolf lying on her bed feels, "[t]he world has changed its shape; the tools of business grown remote... the whole landscape of life lies remote and fair, like the shore seen from a ship far out at sea"(8). The alienated being like 'a ship far out at sea' manages to reflect and re-examine the familiar topography with greater vigour and preciseness.

In illness there is a movement away from the world, a world "so shaped that it echoes every groan" and pain. It is in a way a movement away from a shared being-with-the-world and being-with-the-other. The landscape of health is very different from the landscape of illness. Woolf, in her essay, points out two separate phenomenological conditions— one in health and the other in illness. While in health, "the army of the upright *marches* to battle"; in illness, the recumbent "*float* with sticks on the stream; helter-skelter with the dead leaves on the lawn, irresponsible and disinterested" (12). The more robust *marching* here is in stark contrast to the unstable and unanchored *floating* and *helter-skelter*; the latter being symptomatic of the loosening ties between the self and the world during illness. The body is an anchor through which we are connected to the world; in illness, the anchor itself becomes a burden.

But Woolf in her essay subverts this 'burden hood' of the body in illness into a site of fresh perception. The body in illness, amidst the pain and throbbing, can lead to new horizons which were hitherto unknown and unheard of. She writes, "[...] how astonishing, when the lights of health go down, that undiscovered countries that are then disclosed, what wastes and deserts of the soul a slight attack of influenza bring to light"(3). It can take you to places "where man has not trodden", "where even the print of birds' is unknown" and that enables one with a fresh perspective and new knowledge (15). The kind of epithets she uses in the essay— 'undiscovered', 'virgin', 'unknown' et al.— for the landscape of illness signifies her uncanny existence, her not-being-at-home there. But as already mentioned this not-being-at-home is a de rigueur to any phenomenological perspective. Her going back to the body in-itself then becomes a way of understanding and going back to the things-in-themselves.

The ill body not only gives her a chance to gaze up at the clouds and look sideways on to the world but it also gives her wings of poesy. The way she conceives illness makes her no different from the Romantics and the transcendentalists. As Hermione Lee points out in her 'Introduction', the essay is "at once romantic and modern" (xxvii). The Romantic concept of illness becomes predominant in many parts of the essay and a clear 'anxiety of influence' can easily be traced. Reading in bed, we can trace in her a bit of a reader of Coleridge here and De Quincey there, a bit of Lamb here and Keats there. The antic disposition of the Romantics influences the essay a lot— as if she is half in love with illness and death. Like the Romantics the debilitating illness chariots her to the untrodden landscape of the 'undiscovered countries' and 'virgin forests'. Writing in bed we find in her a recluse— weighed down by fever, fret and weariness— looking for transcendence. In the essay, we see a continuous vacillation between being-ill and becoming-transcendent.

Woolf's vulnerable body takes a radical flight from the binding ontology of totality and perhaps the totality of ontology. Instead of nailing down illness loosens her from the binding existence of 'here, now' providing her a means of escape. As pointed out by Hermione Lee, Woolf writes in her diary that, "The best of these illnesses is that they loosen the earth about the roots. They make changes" (xviii). It pulls her out of her solipsism, her enrootedness and her natural attitude to a domain which is more hospitable and for-the-other. For Levinas vulnerability is a major pre-condition for hospitality; and, for Woolf, this vulnerability comes from her ailing body.

Though she regards illness as 'the great confessional', the virility of the confessional subject is this regard is slackened and humbled by the vulnerability that pain and suffering leads to. Referring to Levinas, Fleurdeliz R. Altez-Albela points out that for him, body is dialectic medium between the existential condition of escape and the condition of a subject struggling against the enrootedness of presence and position[7]. In the case of Woolf, her presence and position were completely overwhelmed by her 'great experience', her pain and illness. They give her the opportunity to undertake a journey, to transcend herself. On being ill brings to her the prospect of 'on going a journey'[8]— a journey towards creating a room of one's own. But not for a long time; the room finally collapses in the year 1941.

This essay was published in 1926 and finally not being able to sustain further, in 1941 she commits suicide. During this period she quite repeatedly acknowledges the overpowering nature of her illness. She finally succumbs to what had made her suffer lifelong. Throughout her lifetime it had controlled almost every aspect of her life. Even her love for her husband was not able to withstand the onslaught. Addressing Leopold Woolf, she writes in her suicide note:

---

[7] For further discussion, see Fleurdeliz R. Altez-Albela, "The Body and Transcendence in Emmanuel Levinas' Phenomenological Ethics", *Kritike Vol.5* (June 2011): 36-50.

[8] The title of the essay echoes William Hazlitt's 1882 essay 'On Going a Journey'. The metaphor of journey becomes a very important one in Woolf's understanding of illness.

Dearest,

I feel certain that I am going mad again. I feel we can't go through another of those terrible times. And I shan't recover this time. I begin to hear voices, and I can't concentrate. So I am doing what seems the best thing to do. You have given me the greatest possible happiness. You have been in every way all that anyone could be. I don't think two people could have been happier 'til this *terrible disease* came. I can't fight any longer. I know that I am spoiling your life, that without me you could work. And you will I know. You see I can't even write this properly. I can't read. What I want to say is I owe all the happiness of my life to you. You have been entirely patient with me and incredibly good. I want to say that — everybody knows it. If anybody could have saved me it would have been you. Everything has gone from me but the certainty of your goodness. I can't go on spoiling your life any longer.

I don't think two people could have been happier than we have been. V.[9]

She considers this 'fight' a lost battle and laments, 'everything has gone from me'. The transcendence and subversion of which she talks about in the essay give way to a more morbid and negative conception of illness as antithetical to love and life. The *journey* finally ends in Rive Ouse into which she submerges herself never to surface again.

Though *On Being Ill* accounts her journey on 'a ship far out at sea' from where the shore of health looks far away the essay also, as Lorraine Sim points out, contrary to the medical discourse of the time "seeks to validate the perspective of the invalid, and while illness and pain are not enjoyable or desirable states Woolf suggests that, as integral aspects of ordinary life, they require much more attention and narrative representation so that as experiences they might be better understood and appreciated"[10]. The *being* of 'on being ill' then ceases to remain a passive being of a patient and turns into a more dynamic *becoming*. Illness leads her to corporeal confinement and spatiotemporal constriction; it also paves the way for a 'radical flight' and transcendence from mechanized existence. Arthur W. Frank deems such journeys/narratives as quest narratives as 'they meet suffering head on'. He observes, "[T]hey accept illness and seek to use it. Illness is the occasion of a

---

[9] Sylvie Crinquand, *Last Letter,* (Cambridge, Cambridge Scholar Publishing, 2009), 43.
[10] Lorraine Sim, *Virginia Woolf: The Patterns of Ordinary Experience,* (Surrey, Ashgate Publishing Limited, 1985), 82.

journey that becomes a quest. What is quested for may never be wholly clear, but the quest is defined by the ill person's belief that something is going to be gained through the experience."[11]

The *telos* of the body is body itself. The *entelechy* of the body is body as *entelechia*. In the essay Woolf's journey to the 'undiscovered countries' is as much bodily as the 'undiscovered country' itself. It is a situation where the space of both the journey and the destination remains the same. Jean Luc-Nancy would consider body to be both 'world' and 'worldling', both 'space' and 'spacing'. This is unlike what Aristotle conceives body to be in the *De Anima*, i.e., soul as the complete realisation or *entelechia* of the body. The *journey* of the body in illness is not merely towards 'presence' in spatial term but, to use Nancy, a 'birth to presence' which is more temporal[12]. This is simply because of its *ek-static* and ever-evolving nature. Derrida would refer to it as touch-without-touching as opposed to simple touch. The 'sense' (body as sense and sense as body) aggravates during illness; and this is what Woolf is trying here to posit. A close reading of the narrative of *On Being Ill* will make it clear that Woolf's depiction of illness is both monadic and nomadic at the same time. Illness enables her to *exscribe* ('writing out') — *from* the body, *to* the body and *through* the body. Her *exscribe* gives us an alternative by thwarting the tendency of modernity to control what Leibniz calls *principium vitale* ('life principle')[13].

Being ill for Woolf is suggestive of a counter-discourse— counter-discursive to the mainstream ideas of modernity. Illness, for her, provides her with a scope of alternative ways of doing modernity. She is modern; there is no iota of doubt as she herself has proclaimed it for her quite a few times. But she is a modern of a different modernity. Her modernity is not machine driven nor is her modernity.

---

[11] Frank, *The Wounded Storyteller*, 115.
[12] It becomes very difficult to speak in terms of simple spatiality or temporality, as Nancy points out in *The Gravity of Thought*, there is no pure space and time but, there are only places, which are simultaneously locations and extensions of bodies; from Jean Luc-Nancy, *The Gravity of Thought: Philosophy and Literary Theory*, (New York, Humanities Press, 1997), 77.
[13] Leibniz writes "This first acting principle, this entelechia is a real life principle (principium vitale) which has a perceiving ability as well, and which is imperishable. And this just what I consider as the soul of animals".

Work Cited

Altez-Albela, Fleurdeliz R. "The Body and Transcendence in Emmanuel Levinas' Phenomenological Ethics". *Kritike Vol. 5.* Web June 2011

Carel, Havi. "The Philosophical Role of Illness". *Metaphilosophy Vol. 45.* 1995: 20-40.

Crinquand, Sylvie (ed.). *Last Letters.* Cambridge: Cambridge Scholar Publishing, 2009.

Frank, Arthur W. *The Wounded Storyteller: Body, Ethics, and Illness.* Chicago: Chicago UP. 1995.

Jean Luc-Nancy, *The Gravity of Thought: Philosophy and Literary Theory,* (New York, Humanities Press, 1997), 77.

Merleu-Ponty, Maurice. *Phenomenology of Perception.* Trans. C. Smith. New York: Routledge, 1962.

Scarry, Elaine. *The Body in Pain: The Making and Unmaking of the World.* Oxford: Oxford UP, 1985.

Sim, Lorraine. *Virginia Woolf: The Patterns of Ordinary Experience.* Surrey: Ashgate Publishing Limited, 2010.

Woolf, Virginia. *A Writer's Diary: Being and Extracts from the Diary of Virginia Woolf.* Ed. Leonard Woolf. San Diego: A Harvest Book, 1954.

Woolf, Virginia. *On Being Ill.* Intro. by Hermione Lee. Massachusetts: Paris Press, 2012.

Chapter 5

'Connect Nothing with Nothing' in T. S. Eliot's *The Wasteland*

> the sickness that must *grow* worse in order to find healing
>
> -Eliot, 'East Coker'

"The physician and the poet", as A. H. Jones points out "can both be healers. They share a common goal in efforts to maintain light and order against the chaos of darkness and disease, and to create or restore the beauty and harmony of health: in this quest, medicine serves the body, poetry the spirit"[1]. T. S. Eliot played the role of a physician in *The Wasteland* masquerading himself in the guise of a poet. And, as a physician, his job was to diagnose the root cause of modernist anxiety and prescribe a prognosis in the form of a new vision of centre. He, in a way, performs one of those Galenic 'radical' surgeries, dissecting the corpse of modern existence only to find out the vacuity that lies underneath the skin. The poem was dedicated to Ezra Pound—'*il miglior fabbro*', the 'better craftsman' or what I call the 'better surgeon'. This dedication gives us an image of Pound performing a surgery upon a poem lying on the table of a dark chamber crying and groaning in agony:

> If you must needs enquire
> Know diligent Reader
> That an inch Occasion
> Ezra performed the Caesarian Operation.[2]

Such an image of 'a patient etherized upon a table' lurks everywhere in the modern period signifying a sudden somatic turn that the early twentieth-century took. This conflation of the *aesthetic* and the *an-aesthetic* can also be viewed as a reversal of Cartesian dualism. The poem diagnoses, as well, an

---

[1] See A.H. Jones, "Literature and Medicine", *The Lancelot Vol. 349*, (1997): 275.
[2] This is the third stanza of a poem titled 'Homme Sage' written by Ezra Pound and included in a letter to Eliot in the late December, 1921 where the former is identifying himelf as the poem's "midwife".

overabundant emphasis on corporeal body and lack of spirituality wherein all the major characters are found to be reduced to their material and decaying body. The Cartesian 'I think therefore, I am' in the poem paves the way for 'I have a body therefore, I am'. Such a reductionist view curtails all other facets of human existence in favour of a process of dehumanization and technologization— characteristic of the modern biopolitical arrangement in which not only is spirituality denied but even bodies are rendered numb and etherized. The modern predicament of *reality* as being reduced to corpo*reality* is something that Eliot is staunchly aware of and can be seen in his portrayal of different bodies in the poem. The modern body and certainly Eliotic numbed body "is stung into sharp, percipient, erotic self-realization by the metropolis, world war, and technology"[3]. Such numbness and an *aesthetic* condition of the modern subject/patient can be traced in the following lines:

> Do
> You know nothing? Do you see nothing? Do you remember
> Nothing? (121-23)

And again,

> Are you alive, or not? Is there nothing in your head? (126)

The modern subjecthood was no different from the patienthood. Both were enjoying the same subject-position and were getting the same kind of *treatment* from the twentieth-century technocratic political and medical establishments both without any voice, agency and autonomy of their own.

The rise of metropolis on one hand and wars on the other reduced the human existence almost to its corporeal existence (*körper*). The gaze which was hitherto *from* the body and *through* the body was now turned upon itself. The body was now its own object and this objectification ultimately led to its alienation and materiality in the modern urban space. In Eliot we see inhospitable bodies existing in an inhospitable space. The Eliotic space is not a body-friendly space and the pathological bodies in the poem find immense difficulty in inhabiting such a hostile environment. Gadamer likens the state of ill-

---

[3] Cassandra Laity, "Decadent Bodies, Modern Visualities, and Changing Modes of Preception", *Modernism/modernity* (2004): 425-448. Project MUSE.

ness to the German word *Gegenstand*[4] as illness— as opposed to health. The former 'objectifies' itself and "confronts us as something opposed to us and which forces itself upon us"[5]. Their being is not with-the-world but rather against-the-world. The wasteland is not inhabited by healthy, porous lived-bodies that are in harmony with the world and which can be "passed-over-in-silence"[6]; the *topos* is inhabited by corporeal, opaque and diseased bodies which "can only connect nothing with nothing". The diseased bodies in the poem are not *ek-statically* involved with the urban space; they are victims of gross mechanization. 'The apparition of these faces in the crowd' and their suffering become quite evident as they somehow drag themselves along the city streets sighing over their condition and living a life of anonymity:

> Unreal City,
> Under the brown fog of a winter dawn,
> A crowd flowed over London Bridge, so many,
> I had not thought death had undone so many.
> Sighs, short and infrequent, were exhaled,
> And each man fixed his eyes before his feet. (60-65)

The urbanity calls for mechanization and, in the poem, we see a machinic portrayal of human existence where on the one hand, machines and tools become prostheses and phantom body parts and, on the other, bodies are portrayed as somnambulistic motors. The dynamic and organic bodies are nowhere to be found in the wasteland. Such conflation of the human and the machine is symptomatic of the process of dehumanization witnessed by the modern era— the body was conceived as a machine just like any other machine, be it a part of a modern metropolis or a modern battleground. Eliot writes,

> At the violet hour, when the eyes and back
> Turn upward from the desk, when the *human engine* waits
> Like a *taxi throbbing* waiting [...] (215-17)

At such a violet hour of modern times, we find subjects *patient*-ly waiting and sighing over their dehumanized existence.

---

[4] Gadamer, *The Enigma of Health*, 105. Gadamer writes, "*Gegenstand* is a highly significant word. It means that which offers resistance (*Widerstand*), that which withstands our natural impulses and which cannot simply incorporate into the order of our lives.
[5] Ibid, 107.
[6] For detailed discussion on the subject, see Jean Paul Sartre, *Being and Nothingness: An Essay on Phenomenological Ontology*, trans. Hazel E. Barnes (London, Routledge, 1958).

The impaired characters in the poem challenges F. H. Bradley's notion of the "felt continuity between the object and oneself"[7]. Bradley in his thesis talks about a common world and a coherent consciousness in harmony with that world. The kind of intersubjectivity and with-the-other existence that he argues for cannot be traced in the wasteland. The Bloomsbury idea of 'only connect' is replaced in the poem by "connect nothing with nothing" (300-301). The latter stands as the condition of illness in which the 'connection' between the being and the world is disrupted. In illness the bridge which was hitherto maintaining the coherent relationship in being-in-the-world and being-with-the-world starts to fall down ["London Bridge is falling down falling down falling down" (427)] leading to insanity ["Hieronymo's mad againe" (432)] and disorder ["Shall I at least set my lands in order?" (432)]. When ill, one can no longer be at ease. The dis-ease that a disease leads to transforms the coherent subject and alienates him/her from the apriori of the life-world. And T. S. Eliot's *The Wasteland* is populated with such characters and situations.

In health, the body remains absent and in illness, this absence comes to the foreground and non-volitionally tries to presence itself. Drew Leder prefers the phrase 'absence of absence' rather than *presence* as the latter brings with it the idea of metaphysics of presence. The disappearing body and that is because of the "body's own tendency toward self-concealment"[8] and its organic involvement with the world is threatened during illness and any such breakdowns. Leder observes that at "moments of breakdown I experience *to* my body, not simply *from* it. My body demands a direct and focal thematization. In contrast to the 'disappearances' that characterize ordinary functioning [in heath], I will term this the principle of *dys-appearance*. That is, the body *appears* as thematic focus, but precisely as in a *dys* state— *dys* is from the Greek prefix signifying 'bad', 'hard', or 'ill', and is found in English words such as 'dysfunctional'"[9]. The dys-appearing bodies of major Eliotic characters like the Cumean Sibyl, Mrs. Equitone, Belladona and her lover, Lil, the typist, Phlebas, Fisher King and most obviously the blind-seer Tiresias forbid them to establish any 'meaningful' connection with the world. They suffer, and their suffering is because of their bodies' dys-appearing. They can now only 'connect nothing with nothing'. It is because of their illnesses (of various

---

[7] Originally from F. H. Bradley's *Appearance and Reality: A Metaphysical Essay;* quoted in Eve Sorum, "Psychology, Psychoanalysis, and New Subjectivities" in *The Cambridge Companion to The Wasteland*, ed. Gabrielle McIntire, (New York, Cambridge University Press. 2015), 164.
[8] See Drew Leder, *The Absent Body*, (Chicago, The University Press of Chicago, 1990), 69.
[9] Ibid, 83-4.

forms) that their connection with the spatiotemporality and especially, the space around is now severed and what remains at the end of the day is:

> A heap of broken images, where the sun beats,
> And the dead tree gives no shelter, the cricket no relief,
> And the dry stone no sound of water. (22-24)

The above lines are the objective correlatives of a pathological condition wherein the sufferer feels not-being-at-home and wherein both the body and the world around cease to remain familiar and become uncanny. It not only leads to a breakdown between the being and the surrounding (in which 'being-there' is replaced by 'being-here') but also a breakdown in the continuum of time— no past, no future but momentary 'here-now'. Both, lived-space and lived-time are constricted and one's condition is pinned down to the level of a 'handful of dust' i.e., the fear of death:

> And I will show you something different from either
> Your shadow at morning striding behind you
> Or your shadow at evening rising to meet you;
> I will show you fear in a handful of dust. (27-30)

Here the 'I' of the narrator points towards a paranoid pathological condition wherein one is cut-off from both 'shadow at morning striding behind you' (i.e., the past) and 'shadow at evening rising to meet you' (i.e., the future) and is reduced as a prisoner of the present without either a discreet 'memory' or 'desire'.

As a matter of fact, in late 1921, Eliot was himself undergoing treatment for his 'nervous breakdown' at a sanatorium near Lake Leman in Lausanne, Switzerland. Matthew K. Gold reads the poem insightfully vis-á-vis Dr. Roger Vittoz' *The Treatment of Neurasthenia By Means of Brain Control* and compares the latter to an "anesthesiologist on call during the delivery, guiding Eliot through the birthing process and slipping him an epidural when the pain became too great. Vittoz' therapeutic programme re-educated Eliot's broken will and enabled him to complete his work. *The Wasteland* stands as a record of Eliot's sickness and his cure"[10]. The references to that mountainous retreat can be traced in lines such as "In the mountains, there you feel free/ I read, much of the night, and go south in winter" (18) and "By the waters of Leman I sat down and wept" (182). Gold lays bare the confluence between poetics and pathology— of how the pathological condition of the creator shapes the poet-

---

[10] Gold, "The Expert Hand and the Obedient Heart", 519.

ic feelings and utterances in a work, and also opens up the possibility of a New Historicist reading of a literary text with the help of a medical treatise. What if the so-called main consciousness behind the poem, as Gold points out, is diagnosed itself as ill— then the whole experience for a reader becomes an exercise towards enlightenment. We would then look at the poem as a text-as-a-sick-body, with a desire or a demand that it could end up revealing something eventually. In a similar vein, if the modern society is portrayed with/as an image of 'a body riddled with sickness', then the possible diagnoses of those ills could prove revelatory and redemptive[11]. *The Wasteland* in this regard "performs a function that is quite similar to the function of Vittoz' book: it educates its readers about their diseased condition and gives them the means to pull themselves out of that condition"[12]. Like Dr. Vittoz, Eliot first tries to diagnose the problem, opening up the cadaver of modern body etherized upon a table and then like any healer looks frantically for the remedy. His restlessness— an antidote to the listlessness of modern human condition— is quite evident in the poem.

The placebos prescribed in the poem are found either in the form of Dr. Vittoz's therapy or F. H. Bradley's ethics or the Buddhist and Upanishadic spiritualism. The loss of wholeness is one of the salient characteristics of illness which he compensates with the 'wholeness' that the above therapeutic, ethical and spiritualist philosophies are to provide. Health, as I have mentioned earlier in my thesis, is often associated with balance and wholeness and it is an illness that leads to the breakdown of this holistic structure. It creates a rupture between the being and the world, the being and the other, mind and body, *körper* and *leib*. And hence, illness on several occasions is deemed a lost wholeness, something that can be traced in Hegel's definition of illness as:

> [...] the system or organ establishes itself in isolation, and by persisting in its particular activity in opposition to activity of the *whole*, obstructs the fluidity of this activity, as well as the process by which it pervades all moments of the *whole*.[13]

Eliot's notion of *Shantih*— 'the peace which passeth understanding'— is very close to the kind of wholeness I am referring. I am also tempted to see this in the light of Gadamer's notion of balance/health; not only this provides a new vision

---

[11] Ibid, 527.
[12] Ibid.
[13] Hegel, G. W. F. Hegel's *Philosophy of Nature*.Vol.3. trans. Michael John Perry. New York, Humanities Press, (1970); quoted from Leder, *The Absent Body*, 88.

of existential centre to the fragmentation and disjuncture of modern sociopolitical condition but also a new vision of health. The latter can act as a placebo and provide some respite to the citizens of the wasteland. The sense of incompleteness and uncanniness that illness brings with it can only be remedied with the help of this new sense of wholeness. "Health", Hans-Georg Gadamer writes, "is a rhythm of life, a continuous process in which balance always stabilizes"[14]. It is this stability, which Eliot frantically looks for throughout the poem.

The Upanishadic utterances *Datta* (give), *Dayadhwam* (sympathise) and *Damayata* (control) also become Eliotic remedies to counter 'the aggressive pathological non-self': and, for that matter, do not advocate a counter-attack in the form of a violent opaque self but rather a hospitable and porous entity in harmony with-the-other. *Datta, Dayadhwam* and *Damayata* do not call for a complete annihilation of self but spaces forth hospitality towards the other. They talk about shared space, a Bradleyan 'common world'— or rather a therapeutic dialogue which Gadamer prescribes with the help of which the disorder and disease can be brought back to the state of balance, harmony and integrality. Taking a cue from Eastern philosophies, Eliot suggests a hospitable and open space where both the sufferer and the healer can come together and be a part of the healing process. This can very well provide a solution for the kind of alienation a patient feels in a modern medical regime. An empathetic and careful understanding can keep at bay the *etherized* condition of the modern patient/subject. A patient hearing of the patient's voice can make the healing process more dialogic and in consonance with the health needs of individuals and collectives. In the poem then Prajapati's voice becomes a catalyst in the process of reclaiming the *voice* of a sufferer.

In such case, 'I cannot' of illness becomes 'I can' and '*have* body' changes into '*am* body'. The disabled conditions of "...I could not/ Speak, and my eyes failed, I was neither/ Living nor dead, and I knew nothing,/ Looking into the heart of the light, the silence" (38-41) are transcended. And here, illness itself plays the role of a catalyst. Because of its telic demand illness not only binds us to the immediate time and space but also generates an overpowering desire to be free from it. This burning desire cannibalizes all other desires and can be compared to the fire of 'The Fire Sermon'. In this section of the poem, Eliot draws heavily from the Fire Sermon preached by Lord Buddha. Leder's understanding of the telic demand can be compared to the Buddhist *tṛṣṇā*. The symbolism of fire in this section not only stands for the truth that there is suffering and a cause of suffering but also, the truth of cessation (*nirodha*) of

---

[14] Gadamer, *The Enigma of Health*, 36.

suffering and the path (*mārga*) of cessation of suffering or liberation (*nirvāna*). The fire in Eliot's poem, hence, embodies the four noble truths or *catvāriārya-satyani* predominant in Buddhist meditations. It not only refers to the raging and uncontrolled fire of passion, the desire that binds us to the wheel of *samsāra* but also to the willed and controlled fire of purification. Following on this argument, we can infer that pain and illness apart from the suffering that they lead to, also give us the opportunity of questioning the 'ignorance is bliss' ideology of a healthy being. Pain and illness initiate a dialogue not only with our own body but also with the world around. This phenomenological distance gives us the room to reflect upon ourselves and also the other. For that moment, they free us from the wheel of *samsāra*. Leder point towards Jean-Paul Sartre and his idea of pain consciousness: "[it] is a project toward a further consciousness which would be empty of all pain; that is, to a consciousness whose contexture, whose being-there would be not painful" and how it can lead to a *hermeneutic* and *pragmatic* moment[15]. This Sartrean 'empty of all pain' can be compared to Eliotic '*Shantih*' and the scriptural 'peace that passeth understanding'.

Now if we go back and re-read the poem, we will see how the images of numb and debilitating effects of disease: "Do/ You know nothing? Do you see nothing? Do you remember/ Nothing?" (121-23) and "Are you alive, or not? Is there nothing in your head?" (126) seem more like phenomenological enquiries. The questions raised are more existential and ontological in nature rather than arbitrary monologues and in all this, illness plays the role of a catalyst. The questions are also very symptomatic of Heideggerian 'concern' (*sorge*) — the kind of questions that a healer may start with in order to start a dialogue with the sufferer, highlighting the fact that *care* is primary to *cure*. As Gadamer points out, "The role of the doctor is to 'treat' or 'handle' the patient with care in a certain manner. The German word treating a patient is *behandeln*, equivalent to the Latin *palpare*. It means, with the hand (*palpus*), carefully and responsively feeling the patient's body so as to confirm or correct the patient's own subjective localization, that is, the patient's experience of pain"[16]. The healer-sufferer relationship ("beating obedient/ to controlling hands") and the responsibility that they should have for each other are epitomized in the following lines wherein Eliot suggests a shared space, a dialogic process that will enable healing humanely— 'reviving for a moment even a broken' boat (read, body):

---

[15] Leder, *The Absent Body*, 77-78.
[16] Gadamer, *The Enigma of Health*, 108.

> The Boat responded
> Gaily, to the hand expert with sail and oar
> The sea was calm, your heart would have responded
> Gaily, when invited, beating obedient
> To controlling hands. (419-23)

The Eliotic diseased bodies are not only incomplete bodies living in a debilitating condition but also ever-unfinished, ambiguous bodies always challenging the notion of the ideal— bodies "that defies clear definitions and borders and that occupies the middle ground between life and death, between subject and object, between one and many"[17]. Eliot himself points out that the condition is 'neither living nor dead'; the epitome of which is Tiresias, phenomenologically *empathetic* 'throbbing between two lives' and *concerned* with a painful knowledge equivalent to 'having foresuffered all'. The *dis-* prefix of the word dis-ease stands for 'apart' and 'away' or in a way distance. This distance (often phenomenological) is what that makes it a philosophical tool through which we can enquire various facets of our existence; somewhat like Eliot's theory of objective criticism. This aspect of illness as 'favourable' and a mode of illumination is something of which even he was aware of, as he writes in 'The Pensées of Pascal',

> [...] not only to religious illumination, but to artistic and literary composition. A piece of writing meditated, apparently without progress, for months or years, may suddenly take shape and word; and in this state long passages may be produced which require little or no retouch.[18]

Illness, therefore, in *The Wasteland*, is both immanent and transcendent in nature. It is as personal as it is civilizational. It is as metaphorical as it is lived. It has been seen not only as the crisis or the symptoms of the crisis but also provides us a method and possibly a solution.

Work Cited

Eliot, T.S. *Selected Prose of T. S. Eliot*. Ed. Frank Kermode. London: Faber and Faber. 1975.

Eliot, T.S. 'The Wasteland'. *The Complete Poems and Plays*. London: Faber and Faber. 1969.

---

[17] Shabot, "Grotesque Bodies", 223-35.
[18] T. S. Eliot, *Selected Prose of T.S. Eliot*, ed. Frank Kermode, (London, Faber and Faber, 1975) 237; quoted in Gold, "The Expert Hand and the Obedient Heart", 527.

Gadamer, Hans-Georg. *The Enigma of Health*. California: Stanford University Press, 1996.

Gold, Mathew K. 'The Expert Hand and the Obedient Heart: Dr.Vittoz, T. S. Eliot, and the Therapeutic Possibilities of *The Wasteland*'. *Journal of Modern Literature*, XXIII, 3-4 (Summer 200). Indianapolis: Indiana Press University. 2001. 519-533.

Jones, A.H. 'Literature and Medicine: Physician-Poets'. *The Lancet Vol. 349*. 1997. 275-278

Laity, Cassandra. Decadent Bodies, Modern Visualities, and Changing Modes of Preception.*Modernism/ modernity* (2004): 11 425-448. Project Muse. 13 Dec 2014.

Leder, Drew. *The Absent Body*. Chicago: The University Press of Chicago, 1990.

Sartre, Jean Paul. *Being and Nothingness: An Essay on Phenomenological Ontology*. Trans. Hazel E. Barnes. London: Routledge. 1958.

Shabot, Sara Cohen. "Grotesque Bodies: A Response to Disembodied Cyborgs". *Journal of Gender Studies*. Vol.15, 2006. pp.223-235.

Epilogue

> Like anyone who has had an extraordinary experience, I wanted to describe it.... My initial experience of illness was a series of disconnected shocks, and my first instinct was to try to bring it under control by turning it into a narrative.
>
> -Anatole Broyard

'To be a body is to be tied to the world'

"To be a body is to be tied to the world" writes Merleau-Ponty[1]. Our bodies act as a bridge between the 'self' and the 'world'— the world is not 'out there' separated from our being but a situation which can easily be deemed as body-in-the-world and body-with-the-world. It is always already embedded, enmeshed and entangled with the world. It is not a product of what Edmund Husserl has called 'intentional feeling' of a self-sovereign ego but, rather, a shared space on the basis of some pre-given world in which we are pre-reflectively involved. However, this constant struggle to keep harmony with the world creates a lot of fissures and these fissures are what make the self fractured and bruised; what remains as residue then at the end of the day are the wounded self and the sadist other. In such a position the body carries the wounds, the signs of conflict between the cultural expectations and personal desire[2]. Since body embodies culture, it becomes, as Elaine Scarry points out, more of a site to carry the scars and the wounds of ideological warfare[3]. Illness then becomes the "unresolved conflict"[4], a broken connection or perhaps a bridge in a dilapidated condition— moving away from what is thought to be the *ideal*.

The inseparability of the body from the surrounding is the state of holiness— the wholeness, completeness and balance— which we call 'health' (etymologically as well as traditionally, the word has been associated with 'holiness'). It is when one is at 'dis-ease' in this interconnectedness that we find a kind of a disjuncture in the harmony. Health is concealed, elusive and enigmatic— a state

---

[1] See Merleau-Ponty, *The Phenomenology of Perception*, 148.
[2] Beth E. Torgerson, *Reading the Brontë Body: Disease, Desire, and the Constraints of Culture*, (New York, Palgrave Macmillan, 2005), 5.
[3] Ibid.
[4] Kleinman, *The Illness Narrative*, 31-32.

of ignorance when one fails to experience the body as a 'thing'. The lived-body (*Leib*), in health, presents itself as a way of being-in-the-world. It is a state of non-dualism where the cogito takes for granted our corporeal existence and, as a consequence, in health, our bodies remain alienated. A dialogue only occurs when there is a sudden rupture between the corporeal body and lived body, the *körper* and the *leib*— it is also the moment my own body becomes the most other— and when one is conscious about one's own body or any of its parts. This state of (ir)reducable gap is violence, a state of 'suffering', a state where we are at dis-ease. This is nothing but a moment of possibility and a ruin of possibility, a proximity and a ruin of proximity.

Our bodies, therefore, are overdetermined all the time; and the overdetermined bodies come with overdetermined suffering and death, biological and cultural both. "Acting like a sponge", Arthur Kleinman observes, "illness soaks up personal and social significance from the world of the sick person" and "absorbs and intensifies life meanings"[5]. The metaphor of sponge gives way to the metaphor of a magnifying glass in illness as it both absorbs the interpersonal and magnifies the personal experiences: beyond the skin and beneath the skin both come into play at that time.

No suffering can ever be away from the lived-body and the lived-experience of the sufferer. A sufferer is too much into the suffering to be separated and read differently. "Illness can be viewed as a clumsy, often misunderstood, a protolanguage' by which I convey my 'dis-ease' with the world. It 'somatizes' my distress over unresolved conflicts. Viewed in this way, the disease is not so much what I have, but what I do. It is a 'surrogate truth', the proper understanding of which can, through guidance, serve as a vehicle for personal liberation from hitherto unresolved life dilemma"[6]. I call this oft-misunderstood protolanguage, in its characteristics, as some form of *ur*-language: a language before language. Thus, to listen carefully to the 'unspoken subject', to the otherwise chaotic and 'nervous narrative' of the 'wounded storyteller', becomes very important. Suffering cannot be de-animated, de-contextualised and de-personalised; the general drama of pain cannot be without its dramatis personae—as a matter of fact "to bypass the patient's *voice* is to bypass the illness itself"[7].

The binary between health and illness, the normal and the abnormal is a constructed one, and there is nothing which is 'natural' in that. Society views

---

[5] Ibid, 97.
[6] See Aho and Aho, *Body Matters*, 61-2.
[7] For strong points of view on the issue, see S. K. Toombs, *The Meaning of Illness: A Phenomenological Account of the Different Perspectives of Physician and Patient*, (Boston, Kluwer Academic Pub, 1992).

health and 'normality' as synonymous and any deviation from 'normality' is deemed to be the opposite to health and to be more precise as sickness—sickness as deviance and deviance as sickness. To the sufferer, the phenomenon manifests as illness (as lived-experience), to the healer as a disease (of the corporeal body) to be cured, and to the society in general as sickness (as some sort of deviance) to be corrected. Although these are three different terms and concepts, in common parlance, they are used interchangeably. The ideas of illness, disease, and sickness are so much enmeshed into each other that it becomes difficult to discuss one without getting influenced by the other. One needs to go beyond the Cartesian dualism of mind and body, illness and disease, in order to understand them properly. These abnormalities, sicknesses and deviations, on the other hand, are also important to maintain the status quo; these phenomena are essential in making the 'normals' feel better about them. Sickness, as Friedrich Nietzsche points out, is so essential for social order and a personal sense of value that if they did not exist, they would have to be invented[8].

Health and illness do not exist in a state of binary. Their existence is together-with existence. They are together and yet different from each other. The germ of illness is 'always already' present in health and vice-versa, i.e., the seed (as a possibility) of health resides in illness all the time. Ruptures in health not only manifest *in* illness but, ruptures in health also *manifest* health, that is, the health as an idea and as an ideal. In illness, the overwhelming desire is that of health. The tendency of health is to make itself absent; and hence, it remains hidden and enigmatic. On the contrary, the tendency of illness is always to be present. Illness *presence* itself and yet remains unrepresentable. Health always tries to repress illness; illness always expresses health. Health *is* when health is denied; and the denial of health is illness. And, it is in this denial that we re-cognise and re-member health. The word re-cognition refers and leads us through the alleys of the past, herein case, an alley that leads us to a long lost home called health. The more prolong the illness remains, the less recognisable the 'home' becomes. The 'home' in chronic ailment becomes 'unhome-like'.

We re-cognise and re-member health only when we are in illness. Illness then is teleological and the telos of illness is health. No journey ensues while we are in health. Health is always in-itself. Illness brings us to the threshold of existence: existence as possibility and possibility as existence. Illness helps us to re-cognise health but in a new way. It brings forth a new understanding of

---

[8] See Aho and Aho, *Body Matters*, 5.

health, not in a customary way but as potentiality-to-be. It challenges the very idea of health being in-itself.

Illness is not a state of exception. Health and illness are not mutually exclusive to each other but to be in illness, as Sontag puts poetically, is like getting a more onerous citizenship of the night-side of life[9]. Each one of us, Sontag writes,

> [...] holds dual citizenship, in the kingdom of the well and in the kingdom of the sick. Although we all prefer to use only the good passport, sooner or later each of us is obliged, at least for a spell, to identify ourselves as citizens of that other place[10].

Illness is not something which is opposed to the 'I'. It lies in the borderline between the self and the not-self. It can rather become a medium to communicate with our own alterity. This tête-à-tête with the other is both loathed and desired at the same time and it is an illness which enables this encounter. An illness, consequently, becomes very essential to our existence so much so that our existence as 'I am' does not remain too far from 'I am ill'. We are ill, 'always, already' ill. There is, therefore, nothing outside-(ill)body. This makes illness as a/an epi/phenomenon very ambivalent and perplexing— a kind of a 'vanishing mediator' between the I and the not-I, life and death, nature and culture, selfhood and dissolution. It is therefore which can be viewed as the 'not not-I' or what, Slavoj Žižek has called *negation of the negation.*

Disease is always followed by the fear of oblivion as for the boundaries of our self and our world begin to collapse. We remain anxious in the face of nothing. It is "the fear of collapse", argues Sander L. Gilman, and "the sense of dissolution" which can only be hindered by the politics of "stigma" or marking, that is, to mark out and objectify those diseased-bodies in the society[11]. The politics of stigma actually enables a being to abstain from collapsing in the face of the Other. So there are some apparatuses, visible and/or invisible, created by the society that serves the dual purpose of dissemination and distancing, both within and without. But such kind of negation (*nichtung*) of the subjectivity is also a mode of self-consciousness. We have occurrences of the ill-other namely, Søren Kierkekaard's Constantine Constantius and Friedrich Nietzsche's Zarathustra who rise like Lazarus from the sickbed with new knowledge and a new lyre. So apart from the politics of biological fragmenta-

---

[9] Sontag, *Illness as Metaphor,* 3.
[10] Ibid.
[11] Sanders L. Gilman, *Disease and Representation: Images of Illness from Madness to AIDS* (Ithaca, Cornell University Press, 1988).

tion, objectification and ghettoisation, this gaze of the other (*le regard*), is also responsible for self-awareness and, especially, general awareness of one's own body. "The Other's look" as Aho and Aho point out, "fashions *my* body in its nakedness, causes it to be born, sculptures it, produces it as it is....The other holds a secret— the secret of what I am"[12]. The mere withdrawal of this gaze can create self-delusion and anxiety.

'There is no outside-body'

The 'history from above' essentially, as I understand, is the 'history from mind'. The 'history from below', in a similar way, could well be envisaged as the 'history from body'. The 'above' has always been thought of to have a mind and the 'below' has always been regarded as to have a body only. This history *from* body is certainly not the history *of* body because of the simple reason that over the course of the period this history *of* body has been seen from and written by the 'above'. The history of body, in that case, is nothing more than a mere façade of the history from above. The only history of body which ought to be taken into consideration is the history of body *from* body and also *through* body. The appropriation of the past through historical essentialism and the appropriation of (ill) body through biological essentialism tend to overlap and overwhelm each other to the extent of becoming almost indistinguishable. The resurfacing of the ill body and a renewed sense of ill body can enable us to a fresh sense of the past. Therefore, as I mentioned earlier in my deliberations on the body— and mostly ill bodies— the body-philosophy writ large: as opposed to the philosophy of body and the body in philosophy. And as I have discussed so far, the varied experiences of the lived reality and the philosophy encircled around those experiences are always, already embodied.

The very absence of body in the metaphysics of presence, or to put it differently, the invisibility of body in western metaphysics is potent enough reason to bring into forth the ill body in our perception of art in general and literature in particular. It is through illness that my body presents itself and it is this presence, and more importantly the very act of presencing, which is capable enough to register a renewed understanding: a new philosophy for understanding the ways, the world and the ways of the world. It can provide us with a tool to understand, of how a way ways.

So, is there a possibility of something as despicable as illness becoming a method of doing philosophy? Is there a possibility where illness can open up new avenues of looking at life? Is there a possibility of illness pulling us out of

---

[12] Aho and Aho, *Body Matters*, 111.

our deep slumber, our state of ignorance? And is there a possibility that all these possibilities can lead us to a renewed conception of illness as distinguished from illness being oft thought as antithetical to the *bliss* of health and life? I think the answer to all these is 'yes'. And especially when it comes to the Modern Period in English literature, these issues become more glaring and such interrogations become more necessary for this was the period when for the first time political surveillance conflated with medical surveillance and, the surveillance of the mind was meted out through surveillance of the body. It is during this period when the bodies— thought of to be inert, passive, static, and reactionary— were objectified, mechanized, dermalised, surveilled, and ghettoized on a massive scale by several discursive practices associated with modernity in general and medical science in particular. The bodies were tattered into pieces and holes were dug into in modern clinics and in modern war-fields, alike. In the fight against the 'other', the bodies were not only used, but most of the time the bodies were themselves turned into the 'other'— the battles were drawn with the bodies and battles were drawn against the bodies. The body emerged as the uncanny 'other' both in political warfare and medical warfare; in the case of the latter, it was specifically the ill body.

The ill body, on the other hand, not only subverts our understanding of mind but also of the body itself (or to be to more exact, the ideal notions of the body). The ill body can prove to be a new method of understanding oneself as well as the world around. The ill body can be read as not only the symptom but also the therapy of modernity. Thinking through ill body helps in disengaging with the different technologies of disciplining: begetting also a much-needed crisis in representation and representationalism. It provides us with alternative ways of being modern and doing modernism. The ill body and the re-making of ill body in our thinking and doing can facilitate us in ways more than one in our making and unmaking of literature.

Works Cited

Aho, James & Aho, Kevin. *Body Matters: A Phenomenology of Sickness, Disease, and Illness*. Plymouth: Lexington Books, 2008.

Gilman. Sanders L. *Disease and Representation: Images of Illness from Madness to AIDS*. Ithaca: Cornell University Press, 1988.

Hawkins, Anne Hunsaker. *Reconstructing Illness: Studies in Illness*. Indiana: Purdue University Press, 1999.

Klienman, Arthur. *The Illness Narrative: Suffering, Healing and the Human Condition*. The US: Basic Book, 1988.

Merleau-Ponty, Maurice. *The Phenomenology of Perception*. Trans. C. Smith. New Jersey: Humanities Press, 1962.

Scarry, Elaine. *The Body in Pain: The Making and Unmaking of the World*. Oxford: Oxford University Press, 1985.

Sontag, Susan. *Illness as Metaphor.* New York: Vintage Books. 1978.
Toombs, S. K. *The Meaning of Illness: A Phenomenological Account of the Different Perspectives of Physician and Patient.* Boston: Kluwer Academic Pub, 1992.

Pathography

Aho, James, and Aho, Kevin. *Body Matters: A Phenomenology of Sickness, Disease, and Illness*. Plymouth: Lexington Books, 2008.

Altez-Albela, Fleurdeliz R. "The Body and Transcendence in Emmanuel Levinas' Phenomenological Ethics". *Kritike Vol. 5*. Web June 2011

Armstrong, Tim. *Modernism, Technology and the Body: A Cultural History*. Cambridge: Cambridge University Press, 1998.

Armstrong, Tim. *Modernism: A Cultural History*. Malden: Polity Press, 2005.

Bair, Deidre. *Samuel Beckett: A Biography*. New York: Touchstone. 1993.

Bakhtin, Mikhail. *Rabelais and His World*. Indianapolis: Indiana Press University, 1965.

Beckett, Samuel. *Endgame & Act Without Words I*. New York: Grove Press, 1957.

Beckett, Samuel. "The Lost Ones". The Complete Short Prose, 1929-1989. New York: Grove Press. 1995.

Benaroyo, L. "The notion of vulnerability in the philosophy of Emmanuel Levinas and its significance for medical ethics and aesthetics", © Lazare Benaroyo, January 2007

Benjamin, Walter. *The Work of Art in the Age of Mechanical Reproduction*. London: Penguin Books Limited, 2008.

Berman, Marshall. *All that is Solid Melts into Air: The Experiences of Modernity*. USA: Penguin Books, 1988.

Blanchot, M. *The Infinite Conversation*. Trans. S. Hanson. Minneapolis: University of Minnesota Press. 1993.

Bourke, Joanna. *The Story of Pain: From Prayers to Painkillers*. Oxford: Oxford University Press, 2014.

Broyard, Anatole. *Intoxicated by My Illness and Other Writings on Life and Death*. Edited by Alexandra Broyard. New York: Clarkson Potter, 1992.

Carel, Havi. "The Philosophical Role of Illness". *Metaphilosophy Vol. 45*. 1995: 20-40. Print.

Carter, Richard. 'The Mask of Thomas Mann (1875-1955): Medical Insights and Last Illness'. The Society of Thoracic Surgeons, Elsevier Science Inc, 1998.

Charon, Rita. *Narrative Medicine: Honoring the Stories of Illness*. New York: Oxford University Press. 2006. Print.

Charon, Rita. 'Narrative Medicine: A Model for Empathy, Reflection, Profession, and Trust'. *JAMA*. October 17, 2001—Vol. 286. No. 15. 1897-1902.

Clewell, Tammy. *Modernism and Nostalgia: Bodies, Locations, Aesthetics*. New York: Palgrave Macmillan. 1993.

Conroy, Colette. *Theatre and the Body*. New York: Palgrave Macmillan. 2010.

Corbin, A. *The Foul and the Fragrant: Odor and the French Social Imagination*. Cambridge: Harvard UP. 1986.

Crawford, T. Hugh. *Modernism, Medicine, and William Carlos Williams*. Norman: University of Oklahoma Press, 1993.

Crinquand, Sylvie (ed.). *Last Letters*. Cambridge: Cambridge Scholar Publishing, 2009. Print

Davidson, Michael (2013): 'By the Road to the Contagious Hospital: Invalid Modernism'. https://www.northumbria.ac.uk/static/.../Lect_4_Fashionable_Diseases.pdf (November 10, 2013)

Eliot, T. S. Eliot. *The Complete Poems and Plays of T. S. Eliot*. London: Faber & Faber, 1969.

Eliot, T.S. *Selected Prose of T. S. Eliot*. Ed. Frank Kermode. London: Faber and Faber. 1975.

Elvin, Mark. "A Working Definition of 'Modernity'?" *Past & Present*, no. 113, 1986, pp. 209–213. www.jstor.org/stable/650986

Foucault, Michel. *The Birth of the Clinic*. London: Routledge, 1997.

Frank, Arthur W. *The Wounded Storyteller: Body, Illness, and Ethics*. Chicago: The University of Chicago Press, 1995.

Gadamer, Hans-Georg. *The Enigma of Health: The Art of Healing in a Scientific Age*. California: Stanford University Press, 1996.

Gawande, Atul. *Being Mortal: Medicine and What Matters in the End*. India: Hamish Hamilton. 2014.

Gilman, Sander. *Difference and Pathology. Stereotypes of Sexuality, Race, and Madness*. Ithaca: Cornell University Press, 1985.

Gilman. Sanders L. *Disease and Representation: Images of Illness from Madness to AIDS*. Ithaca: Cornell University Press, 1988.

Gilman, Sander. *Franz Kafka, the Jewish Patient*. London: Routledge, 1995.

Gilman, Sander L. *Franz Kafka: Critical Lives*. London: Reaktion Books. 2005.

Ghosh. Ranjan. 'Reading and Experiencing a Play Transculturally'. *Comparative Drama Vol. 45 No. 3*. Michigan: Western Michigan University, 2012. 260-281.

Gold, Mathew K. 'The Expert Hand and the Obedient Heart: Dr.Vittoz, T. S. Eliot, and the Therapeutic Possibilities of *The Wasteland*'. *Journal of Modern Literature*, XXIII, 3-4 (Summer 200). Indianapolis: Indiana Press University. 2001. 519-533.

Gosetti-Ferencei, Jennifer Anna. 'Death and Authenticity: Reflections on Heidegger, Rilke, Blanchot'. *Existenz Vol. 9/1*, 2014. 53-62.

Gubar, Susan. *Memoir of a Debulked Woman*. New York: W. W. Norton & Company, 2012.

Harris, Jonathan Gill. *The First Firangis: Remarkable Stories of Heroes, Healers, Charlatans, Courtesans and other Foreigners who Became Indian*. India: Aleph Books. 2015.

Hawkins, Anne Hunsaker. *Reconstructing Illness: Studies in Illness*. Indiana: Purdue University Press, 1999.

Heidegger, Martin. *Being and Time. A Translation of Sein and Zeit*. Trans. Joan Stambaugh. Albany: State University of New York Press, 1996.

Heidegger, Martin. *Zollikon Seminars: Protocols-Conversations-Letters*. Ed. Medard Boss. Illinois: Northwestern University Press, 1987.

Hennezel, Marie de. *Seize the Day: How the Dying teach us to live.* Trans. Carol Brown Janeway. London: Pan Macmillan, 2012.

Howells, Christina. *The Cambridge Companion to Sartre.* Cambridge: Cambridge University Press, 1992.

Jones, A.H. 'Literature and Medicine: Physician-Poets'. The Lancet Vol. 349. 1997. 275-278

Kafka, Franz. *Letters to Friends, Family, and Editors,* Ed. Max Brod. Trans. James stern and Elisabeth Duckworth. New York: Schocken, 1977.

Kafka, Franz. *Letters to Felice.* Ed. Erich Heller and Jurgen Born. Trans. James Stern and Elizabeth Duckworth. New York: Schocken. 1973.

Kafka, F. *Letters to Milena.* Trans. Philip Boehm. New York: Schocken, 1990.

Kafka, F., Muir, E., and Muir, W. *The Penal Colony, Stories and Short Pieces.* New York: Schocken Books, 1976.

Kafka, Franz. *Letters to Ottla and the Family.* Ed. N. N. Glatzer. Trans. Richard and Clara Winston. New York: Schocken. 1982.

Kakkar, Sudhir (ed). *Death and Dying.* India: Penguin Books, 2012.

Kierkegaard, Søren. *Concluding Unscientific Postscript.* Trans. Alastair Hannay. Cambridge: Cambridge University Press, 2009.

Kierkegaard, Søren. *The Sickness unto Death: A Christian Psychological Exposition of Edification and Awakening by Anti-Climacus.* Trans. Alastair Hannay. UK: Penguin Books. 2004.

Klienman, Arthur. *The Illness Narrative: Suffering, Healing and the Human Condition.* The US: Basic Book

Koelb, Clayton. *Thomas Mann's 'Goethe and Tolstoy': Notes and Sources.* Alabama: The University of Alabama Press. 1984. 205.

Laity, Cassandra. Decadent Bodies, Modern Visualities, and Changing Modes of Preception. *Modernism/ modernity* (2004): 11 425-448. Project Muse. 13 Dec 2014.

Leder, Drew. *The Absent Body.* Chicago: The University Press of Chicago, 1990.

Lefkovitz, Lori Hope. *Textual Bodies: Changing Boundaries of Literary Represention.* Albany: SUNY, 1997.

Levinas, Emmanuel. *Otherwise than Being or Beyond Essence.* Trans. Alphonso Lingis. The Netherlands: Kluwer Academic Press. 1981.

Levin, David M. 'Mudra as Thinking: Developing Our Wisdom-of-Being in Gestures and Movements' in Parkes. Graham. *Heidegger and Asian Thought.* Delhi: Motilal Banarsidas Publishers, 2010. 245-270.

Levinas, Emmanuel. *Existence and Existents.* The Hague: Nijhoff. 1978.

Long, Lisa A. *Rehabilitating Bodies: Health, History and the American Civil War,* Pennsylvania: University of Pennsylvania, 2004.

Lupton, Deborah. *Medicine as Culture: Illness, Disease and the Body in Western Societies.* London: Sage Publication, 1994.

Mann, Thomas. *Thomas Mann's "Goethe and Tolstoy": Notes and Sources.* Ed. Clayton Koelb. Alabama: University of Alabama Press, 1984.

Mann, Thomas. *The Magic Mountain,* Trans. H. T. Lowe Porter. London: Vintage, 1999.

Mann, Thomas. *Death in Venice.* Trans. Michael Henry Heim. New York: Harper Collins, 2004.

McEntyre, Marilyn Chandler. *Patient Poets: Illness from Inside Out.* San Francisco: University of California Medical Humanities Press, 2012.

McNeill, William H. *Plagues and Peoples.* New York: Quality Paperbacks, 1993.

Merleau-Ponty, Maurice. *The Visible and the Invisible.* Evanston: Northwestern University Press, 1968.

Merleau-Ponty, Maurice. *The Phenomenology of Perception.* Trans. C. Smith. New Jersey: Humanities Press, 1962.

Merleau-Ponty, Maurice. *The Visible and the Invisible.* Evanston: Northwestern University Press, 1968.

Nancy, Jean Luc. *Being Singular Plural.* Trans. Robert D. Richardson and Anne E. O'Byrne. Stanford: Stanford University Press, 2000.

Nancy, Jean-Luc. *Corpus.* Trans. Richard Rand. New York: Fordham University Press, 2008.

Nietzsche, Friedrich. *The Gay Science.* trans. Walter Kaufmann. New York: Vintage, 1974.

Porter, Roy. *Flesh in the Age of Reason.* New York: W. W. Norton & Company, 2003.

Quayson, Ato. *Aesthetic Nervousness: Disability and the Crisis of Representation.* New York: Columbia University Press, 2007.

Rau, Petra. *Bodies-at-War: Conflict, Nationhood and Corporeality in Modern Literature.* New York: Palgrave Macmillan, 2010.

Robertson, Ritchie. *The Cambridge Companion to Thomas Mann.* Cambridge: Cambridge University Press, 2004.

Sanders, Lisa. *Every Patient Tells a Story: Medical Mysteries and the Art of Diagnosis.* New York: Broadway Books, 2009.

Sartre, Jean Paul. *Being and Nothingness: An Essay on Phenomenological Ontology.* Trans. Hazel E. Barnes. London: Routledge, 1958.

Sartre, Jean-Paul. *No Exit and The Flies.* New York: Knopf. 1946.

Scarry, Elaine. *The Body in Pain: The Making and Unmaking of the World.* Oxford: Oxford University Press, 1985.

Shabot, Sara Cohen. "Grotesque Bodies: A Response to Disembodied Cyborgs". *Journal of Gender Studies.* Vol.15, 2006. pp.223-235.

Sheehan, Paul. *Modernism, Narrative and Humanism.* UK: Cambridge University Press. 2004.

Sim, Lorraine. *Virginia Woolf: The Patterns of Ordinary Experience.* Surrey: Ashgate Publishing Limited. 2010.

Slaterry, Dennis Patrick. *The Wounded Body: Remembering the Markings of Flesh.* Albany: SUNY, 2000.

Sontag, Susan. AIDS and Its Metaphors. New York: Farrar, Strauss and Giroux, 1988.

Sontag, Susan. *Illness as Metaphor.* New York: Vintage Books. 1978.

Swanson, Victoria. Confining, Incapacitating, and Partitioning the Body: Carcerality and Surveillance in Samuel Beckett's *Endgame, Happy Days,* and

Play. in Miranda [Online]. Université Toulouse. http://miranda.revues.org/. 2011.

Toombs, S. K. *The Meaning of Illness: A Phenomenological Account of the Different Perspectives of Physician and Patient.* Boston: Kluwer Academic Pub, 1992.

Torgerson, Beth E. *Reading the Brontë Body: Disease, Desire, and the Constraints of Culture.* New York: Palgrave Macmillan, 2005.

Williams, William Carlos. *The Doctor Stories.* New York: A New Directions Book, 1984.

Williams, M. J. Teasdale, Z. Segal, and J. Kabat-Zinn. *The Mindful Waythrough Depression: Freeing Yourself from Chronic Unhappiness.* New York: The Guilford Press, 2007.

Weber, Max. *The Protestant Ethic and the Spirit of Capitalism.* New York: Dover Publications, 2012.

Woolf, Virginia. *A Writer's Diary: Being and Extracts from the Diary of Virginia Woolf.* Ed. Leonard Woolf. San Diego: A Harvest Book. 1954.

Woolf, Virginia. *On Being Ill.* Intro. by Hermione Lee. Massachusetts: Paris Press, 2012.

Index

A

Adorno, Theodor 2
Aho, James and Kevin xxvi, xxxix, 1, 6, 7, 13, 63, 64
alētheia (truth) xxviii
anamnēsis 11, xxviii
angst 23, ix, x, xxi, xxii, xxxiii, xxxv
Anti-Semite xiii, xxxiv, 17
Apollonian 27, 32, 33, 35
Apollinaire, Guillaume xxiii
Aristotle 46
Armstrong, Tim ix, xxiii, xxxix
Arnold, Mathew xxv
ars moriendi ("art of dying") xxxii, xxxvi
Auden, W. H. xxiv

B

Bakhtin, Mikhail xxxix, 23, 25
balance 5, 54, 55, 59
Baudelaire, Charles xxv
Bauer, Felice 15, 16
Beckett, Samuel ix, xiv, xx, xxxii, xxxiii, xxxiv, 1-14
beckettesque xxxiv, 4, 11, 12
Being and Nothingness xix, 23, 26, 51, 58
Being and Time 35, 36
Benjamin, Walter xxi, xxxix
Bergson, Henri 33, 36
Blanchot, Maurice 21, 25, 35, 36
Body Dysmorphic Disorder (BDD) xxxviii, 17
Body-for-other 16, 18
Bradley, F. H. 52, 54, 55
Brod, Max xl, 15, 18, 19, 24, 25
Buddhism 54, 55, 56
BwO 15

C

Cartesian dualism xxi, xxvii, 49, 61
catvāriārya-satyani 56
Charon, Rita xxviii, xxix, xxxix
cholera xiv, xxxvi, xxxviii, 27, 29, 32
Classicism 33
Coleridge, Samuel Taylor 43
corporealization 17
Corpus xxiii, xl, 24, 26
corpse xxiii, 49

D

Dasein (being-there) xxviii, 22, 31, 35
De Anima 46
death xiii, xiv, xix, xx, xxv, xxvii, xxxi, xxxii, xxxv, xxxvi, 23, 24, 27-9, 32-6, 53, 57, 58, 60, 62
Death in Venice xiii, xiv, xxxii, xxxvi, xl, 27-37
Deleuze, Gilles 15, 25
de/territorialization xxxv, 21
depaysement ix, xiv, xxxvi, 28
Derrida, Jacques xxvi, 31, 46
despair xxxi, xxxii
disability xiii, xx, xxvi, xxviii, xxix, xxxiv, xxxxi, 2, 3, 5-7, 9,11, 12, 13
disenchantment xxxi
de-worldling 31
differancé xxvi
difference xix, xxvi, 15, 23, 42

Dilthey, William xxvi
Dionysian xiv, xxxvi, 27, 30, 32, 33, 34
disharmony 42
Dostoevsky, Fyodor xxv
Dr. Vittoz, Roger xxxix, 54, 58
dying xiii, xiv, xix, xxxvii, 27, 29, 34, 35, 36

E

ek-static 46, 51
Eliot, T. S. ix, x, xiii, xiv, xx, xxvi, xxxii, xxxiii, xxxvii, xxxviii, xl, 49-58
élan vital 36
Endgame xii, xxxii, xxxiv, xxxix, 1-14
entelechy 46
epoché xiv, xxxvii, 42
erziehung 29
exscribe ("writing out") 46

F

fin-de-siècle xxxv, 21
flesh xiii, xiv, xx, xxxv, 22, 23, 25
foreign ix, xiv, xxxvi, 16, 18, 28, 29, 31,
Foucault, Michel xxxix, 1, 36
Frank, Arthur W. 30, 36, 39, 45, 46, 47, 57

G

Gadamer, Hans-Georg xxxix, 32, 36, 50, 51, 54, 55, 56, 58
Galen 49
Gilman, Sander 62, 64
grotesque xxxv, 1, 23, 40, 41
Guattari, Felix 15, 25
Gumbrecht, Hans Ulrich 24

H

harmony 18, 19, 33, 42, 49, 51, 52, 55, 59
Hawkins, Anne Hunsaker xx, xxxiii, 36
Hegel, G. W. F. 54
Heidegger, Martin xiii, xix, xxvii, xxviii, xxix, 31, 35, 36, 56
Holocaust xxiii, xxxii, xxxiv, 3
Husserl, Edmund xxix, 41, 42, 59

I

impairment xxi, xxxiv, 3, 4, 6, 7, 8, 11, 13

J

Jew xxxv, 15, 16, 21,
Jewish body xxiii, xxxiv, xxxv, 17, 21, 23, 24

K

Kafka, Franz ix, xxiii, xx, xxxii, xxxiii, xxxiv, xxxv, xxxvii, xxxix, xl, 15-25,
Kafkaesque 19, 36
Keats, John 34
Kleinman, Arthur 59, 60,
Kierkegaard, Søren xxv, xxxi, xxxii, xl, 35, 69
körper (corporeal body) 6, 18, 50, 54, 60

L

La Mettrie 7
Leavis, F. R. xx
Lebenswelt (life-world) xxvii
Leder, Drew xxii, xl, 52, 54, 55, 56
Lee, Hermione 43, 44

Index

leib (lived-body) 18, 41, 46, 54, 60
Leibniz, G. W. 46
Levinas, Emmanuel xxiii, xix, 22, 25, 44
lived-space xxxiv, 6, 7, 35, 53
lived-time xxxiv, 7, 53
lived-experience xxxiii, 60, 61
Lorde, Audrey 30
Luc-Nancy, Jean xxiii, xix, xxiii, xxix, 24, 46

M

machine xiv, xxxvii, 1, 7, 24, 31, 46, 51
Mann, Thomas ix, x, xiii, xiv, xx, xxi, xxxii, xxxiii, xxxiv, xxxvi, xxxvii, 27- 47
Marinetti, F. T. xxi,
mārga 56
medicine xxi, xxxv, xxxvi, 25, 40, 49
medical death 36
melancholia 35
melete thanatou 33
Merleau-Ponty, Maurice x, xiii, xix, xxix, 6, 23, 42, 59
mind, xiv, xix, xx, xxi, xxiii, xxiv, xxvi, xxvii, xxx, xxxi, xxxii, xxxiv, xxxviii, 21, 27, 34, 39, 41, 54, 61, 63, 64
modernism ix, x, xiv, xv, xxii, xxiii, xxv, xxvi, xxx, xxxi, xxxviii, 64
modernity xiii, xiv, xv, xx, xxii, xxiii, xxiv, xxvi, xxviii, xxx, xxxi, xxxii, xxxii, xxxiv, xxxvii, xxxviii, 36, 46, 50, 64
mourning 35

N

narrative medicine xxviii, xxix
nichtung (negation) 22, 62

Nietzsche, Fredrich xxv, 12, 61, 62
nirodha 55
nostalgia xxii

O

On Being Ill xxii,
On Going a Journey xxxvii, 44
ousia 25

P

pain xxiii, xv, xix, xx, xxi, xxvii, xxviii, xxx, xxxi, xxxiv, 1, 2, 8, 9-13, 19, 22, 23, 24, 30, 31, 33, 39, 40, 41, 43, 44, 45, 53, 56, 60
palpare 56
pathography ix, xv, xx, xxxii, xxxiii
pathological xiv, xxii, xxvii, xxxvii, 16, 21, 24, 35, 50, 53, 55
patient xv, xix, xxi, xxiii, xxiv, xxix, xxx, xxxiii, 20, 21, 45, 49-51, 55, 56
pharmakon xxvi
phenomenology xxiii, xx, xxvii, 1, 24
Picasso, Pablo xxiii, xxvi
Plato 33, 35
poena 24
poetics xiii, xiv, xix, xxi, xxvii, 15, 16, 23, 36, 53
poiesis xv, xx, xxxii
potentiality-for-being 35
Pound, Ezra x, xxv, 49
Prajapati 55
praktognosia 6
principium vitale 46

Q

Quayson, Ato 1, 2, 3, 8, 11, 12, 13

R

res extensa xxii
Romantics xxxvii, 34, 43, 44

S

samsāra 56
Sartre, Jean Paul xxiii, xix, xxix, 3, 4, 5, 23, 26, 51, 56, 58
Scarry, Elaine x, xl, 10, 13, 31, 40, 47, 59, 64
Schopenhauer, Arthur 30
Shoah xiii, xxxv, 23
sickness xiv, xxv, xxxi, xxxvi, xxxvii, xxxviii, 49, 53, 54, 61
somatic turn xiii, xx, xxxiii, xxxv, 25, 49
Sontag, Susan x, xl, 15, 16, 21, 26, 32, 62, 65
sorge 56
soul xxvi, 22, 30, 33, 34, 41, 43, 46

T

telic demand xxii, 55
The Magic Mountain xxxvi, xl, 30, 34, 37,
'The Penal Colony' xxxv, xl, 23
The Phenomenology of Perception 59, 64
The Wasteland xxiii, xxxii, xxxvii, xxxviii, xxxix, 49-58
transcendental xxiii, xxvii, 43
transcendentalism 39, 43
trsnā (desire) 55
tuberculosis xxxv, xxxvi, xxxviii, 15, 16, 17, 20, 21, 23

U

ungeheur 32

unheimlich (uncanny) xxvi
Upanishad 54, 55

V

Victorian xxxv
Vittoz, Dr. Roger xxxviii, xxxix, 53, 54, 58
Volkskorper 18

W

Wagner xxvi
War xx, xxi, xxxii, xxxiv, 16, 17
Williams, William Carlos 39
Woolf, Leopold 44
Woolf, Virginia ix, x, xiii, xiv, xx, xxiii, xxxii, xxxiii, xxxvii, xl, 39-47

Z

Žižek, Slavoj 62

www.ingramcontent.com/pod-product-compliance
Lightning Source LLC
Chambersburg PA
CBHW051529230426
43668CB00012B/1788